Getting to the Heart of Your Child

Peggy Hughes

"Peggy Hughes is a devoted wife, mother of two adult children, and an insightful Christian counselor. She uses her personal and counseling experience to deliver a very helpful and practical book for parents. In *Getting to the Heart of Your Child*, she explains how and why building strong and trusting relationships with your children is the key to raising godly men and women. As a mother of six children myself, I could have benefitted greatly from this book many years ago. There is such a need for godly wisdom and biblical truth to be instilled into parents today, when so much worldly "wisdom" (which is really foolishness) is pulling families apart. I highly recommend that parents read and apply the principles of this book, wherever they are on their journey of parenting."

—Jennifer Benes
Wife of former St. Louis Cardinals' pitcher,
Andy Benes

"*Getting to the Heart of Your Child* is a book that all parents, especially those expecting a child, should read. The advice is biblical and very practical. I wish this book would have been available for my wife and me when we first became parents. The stories Peggy shares about her own experiences as a parent are relatable to all. What a wonderful help!"

—Kenny Sims
Senior Pastor at *Raintree Church*,
Hillsboro, Missouri

"This is a book every parent should read to do a reality check on where you are as a parent. It will help you discover how to effectively reach and train the heart of your child. I recommend this book to the parents I work with as a counselor."

—Dave Holden
M.Div., MAC, LPC,
Genesis Christian Counseling

"Peggy Hughes truly has a heart for parents and their children! Her formula regarding rules and relationships for rearing a healthy, non-rebellious child by utilizing loving, consistent discipline is built on sound advice. Her poignant, personal stories and bittersweet remembrances from her own childhood challenge us to observe, communicate, and cultivate our own ever-so-important parent/child relationships. God blessed us by making us parents. Peggy reminds us that it's never too late to be the best one we can be!"

—Julie Norris
Author and Speaker

"Through a unique blend of practical, biblical truths and real-life stories, Peggy offers parents timeless principles that work. As a father of four, I really appreciate the balance she provides between building a loving relationship with our kids and establishing and maintaining rules. Well done, Peggy!

—Vincent M. Newfield
Author, Communicator, Minister,
New Fields Creative Services

EDITOR AND CONCEPT DEVELOPMENT:
Vincent M. Newfield, New Fields & Company
P. O. Box 622, Hillsboro, Missouri 63050
www.newfieldscreativeservices.com

INTERIOR DESIGN:
Lisa Simpson, Simpson Productions
www.SimpsonProductions.net

COVER DESIGN: Wesley Goldsborough
Divinedesign.us

Dedication

This book is dedicated to Harold and Helen Holloway who demonstrated unconditional love and gentle discipline as they surrounded all they did in godly wisdom. I am so very grateful to have had them as my parents. I would also like to dedicate this book to my husband, Don, and our children, Stephanie Read and Alan Hughes.

Acknowledgments

Thank you to my wonderful husband, Don, and children, Stephanie Read and Alan Hughes who have willingly allowed our family's stories to be shared with strangers. Your encouragement and support through the years has enabled me to write this book. Don, thanks for supporting me as you came home day after day only to see me at the computer still in my pj's, convincing myself I was really going to finish this project.

Stephanie and Alan, I am so proud of you both! Without your support and permission to be vulnerable, we would never have this book. I am so thankful for your heart for others and your passion for the Lord in all you do!

I would also like to thank Dave Holden, my co-founder of Genesis Christian Counseling, for his teachings on the heart. Although I grew up with this premise and we raised our children in this way, he helped bring light to the practical explanation of the importance of the heart.

I would also like to thank Vincent and Allison Newfield for their insightful editing. They quickly grabbed onto the premise and passion of this book and helped it become a reality.

And to our Lord and Savior who cares so very deeply about our children and our relationship with Him. I am only a foot soldier in His great and loving army. He is our all-loving, all-powerful Commander in Chief. To Him be the honor and the glory!

Contents

Introduction

How Do I Do
This Parenting Thing?

When we found out I was pregnant, it was an exciting day! My husband, Don, and I had tried for several years to conceive, but to no avail. Our first pregnancy ended in a miscarriage, and we were heartbroken. Nine months later, we learned that I was pregnant again. Time marched on, and as we drew closer to the due date, it dawned on me that I really was going to be a mommy. It also dawned on me that I had never been a mommy before. I had *no* experience with babies or young children, and I found myself fighting panic.

Immediately, I began reading every parenting book I could find. I read oodles of information on bathing and feeding a baby, but I could not find a single book guaranteeing that I would be a great mom if I only followed a few simple steps. I was in search of a "Parenting for Dummies" type of book. Not finding it, I was pretty much on my own. (Good luck with that!)

Proverbs 22:6 instructs us to, "Train up a child in the way he should go, and when he is old he will not depart from it" (NKJV). I had read this verse multiple times in my life, but now as an expectant mom, it took on new meaning. I knew it was not a guarantee, but a probability. In other words, if we train up our children in the way they should go, we have a much better chance of them going in the right direction.

Again and again, I read this verse. Each time my intrigue deepened. *How do we "train up" a child?* I thought. *And where are they supposed to "go"?*

Before we knew it, our baby arrived. Not long after that, our second one came. Stephanie and Alan were the most precious bundles of joy my husband and I had ever laid eyes on. As we stared down on each of them, we continued to ask ourselves those questions—but now it was personal. *How do we train up **our** children? And where should they "go"?* What a blessing they were and a responsibility they would be!

Indeed, it is an awesome responsibility to raise children. Don and I realized that we had very little to do with Stephanie and Alan's existence! Their lives were predetermined by a higher authority than us. Their DNA, personality, health, entrance into this world, and everything about them was unique and divinely ordered. These things were impossible for us to determine or create. Therefore, they were not really ours, but loaned to us from God! He had given us a huge responsibility, appointing us to be their parents, protectors, and providers. We were not chosen to merely babysit them, but to raise them "in the way they should go."

Personally, I found that rather intimidating. However, I knew the Lord did not just drop them off at our doorstep and wish us the best of luck. He promised to never leave us or forsake us. When we seek God's direction and wisdom, He promises to always guide us—including our journey through the parenting process. He says, "I will instruct you and teach you in the way you should go; I will counsel you and watch over you" (Psalm 32:8).

Don and I enjoyed the children the Lord gave us and committed to cherish every new stage of their lives. A number of parents warned us, "Take time to enjoy them. Before you know it, they will grow up and fly away." Realizing our family would be no exception to this rule, I kept these words in mind.

I truly loved the baby stage, when I was in control and there was no discipline needed. The only thing they required was lots of love and physical care. I took advantage of their infantile thoughts that I was the most important person in their lives. I wanted to keep that going as long as possible. But as they grew older, I realized I had to deal with God's instruction to "train them up in the way they should go." This was still confusing me.

Have you ever considered that instruction? Do you know what it means to "train up your child"? And what is "the way they should go"? If you don't know where they should go, it certainly is a challenge to know how to get them there!

In order to answer these questions, you need to look further down the road from where you are right now. Stop and think. What type of individual has God wired your child to be? Who should they become? For Don and me, we desired our children to become responsible, good citizens who respected and loved others. We wanted them to be good students and good employees (and/or good employers). We wanted them to think on their own and be leaders. And we wanted them to experience the Lord's love, peace, and direction for their lives.

If you have not wrestled with these questions, I encourage you to do so. Let the answers be your goal in parenting and your reason to do what you do when you parent.

In *Getting to the Heart of Your Child*, we will take a look at ways to answer these questions. We will peer into God's Word and see how His practical principles apply to raising our children.

We will also learn how vital it is to know the heart of your child in order to help them get to where they need to go.

Along the way, I will share some stories from our family as well as from other families that have already faced some of the challenges you may be facing right now. I hope you will enjoy them, learn from them, and share in our joy, our laughter, and our tears.

WHY IS PARENTING SO RELEVANT?

Do you remember the fairy tale "Little Red Riding Hood"? When it comes to parenting, it contains some valuable principles that are worth our attention. A quick paraphrase of the story would be something like this…

> "Once upon a time, there was a little girl named Red who lived in a village near the forest. One day, Little Red Riding Hood, as she was called, asked her mother if she could go visit her grandmother.
>
> 'That's a nice idea,' her mother said. They then packed a picnic basket filled with goodies for her to take to her grandmother's house. 'Be careful,' the mother warned. 'Don't dally and don't talk to strangers. Go straight there. The woods can be very dangerous.'
>
> 'Don't worry mommy. I'll be careful,' the little girl replied, as she set off for grandmother's house. But as Little Red Riding Hood journeyed through the woods, she noticed some pretty flowers. She soon forgot her promise to her mother and stopped to pick a few. For quite some time, she sat and watched the butterflies play and picked flower after flower. She was so busy enjoying

her surroundings that she did not notice the large shadow approaching from out of the forest behind her.

Suddenly, a wolf appeared and startled her. 'What are you doing out here little girl?' the wolf asked in the most friendly voice he could muster.

'I'm going to my grandmother's house,' Red replied. 'She lives in the forest next to the brook.' With that, she realized how late she was and quickly headed to her grand- mother's. The cunning wolf knew a short cut through the woods and quickly took it. He found the grandmother's house, went in, and ate poor grandma. When Little Red Riding Hood arrived, the wolf had disguised himself as her sweet grandmother. Although something didn't seem quite right to the little girl, she engaged her 'grandmother' in conversation.

'My, what big ears you have, grandmother!' she exclaimed.

'All the better to hear you with, my dear,' the wolf lovingly responded. As the questions ensued, Red came closer and closer to the one she thought was her loving grandmother. Suddenly and without warning, the ill- intentioned wolf snatched Red and gobbled her up."

Poor Little Red. She was a lovely girl filled with great potential and good thoughts. But she got entangled with an evil creature who disguised himself as her loving grandmother. Even though her mother warned her, she was enticed by all things beautiful. She forgot her mother's warning of stranger danger and her instruction to go straight to her grandmother's. When she finally arrived, her curiosity prevailed. Deceived and in great danger, she moved closer to the evil wolf and is eaten.

And what about poor mom? Can you relate to her? She loved her daughter and appreciated her compassion toward her grandmother. She also knew her little girl was naïve and unaware of the dangers that were out there. So she sent her off with her blessing and a warning: "Watch out on the path you are taking. I know it looks lovely, but it can be a dangerous one. Go straight to grandma's house. Don't be distracted by anything or deceived by anyone!" But Red did not heed her instruction.

As a parent, you are raising your own "Little Red Riding Hoods." Like Red, your children set out on a journey having good intentions. Their path is paved with promise, and their hearts are filled with innocence and wonder as they travel through life. They do not know that there is a "big bad wolf" ahead, plotting harm against them. Instead, they are enticed by things that look appealing and enjoyable.

Like the wolf in the story, their enemy knows that if he shows his true self to your kids, they will instantly recognize him and run away. Therefore, he chooses to disguise himself as something that they love. They are provided with paths full of distractions that are laced with hidden trouble. The trouble disguises itself as something harmless and inviting. It doesn't show its true colors until it is too late. Deception is the chosen tool to put your kids in harm's way!

Indeed, our culture has dramatically changed in the past thirty years from what it once was. It provides our children with so many more paths to choose from than Little Red Riding Hood. These paths are disguised to entice, yet designed to harm. The fact is, we are experiencing a societal evolution, and our children need us now more than ever to train them and guide them in the way they should go.

Your role as a parent is *crucial!* God has called you and positioned you to protect your own Little Reds from being ensnared by the potential dangers that are coming their way. They don't have to look for it; it is right under their noses. To discern what is ahead and give them what they need, you must *get to know their heart.*

Part I:

Understanding the Right Foundation

"A joyful heart is the inevitable result of a heart burning with love."

—Mother Teresa[1]

The Importance of the Heart

"Above all else, guard your heart,
for it is the wellspring of life."
Proverbs 4:23

One of my favorite places to visit in Missouri is the town of Eminence. It is home to many gorgeous springs that feed the Jacks Fork River. Some of them rank among the largest springs in the world. Sitting by these springs and watching the water bubble out of the ground truly amazes me. To think of the constant flow of all that water pouring into and feeding the Jacks Fork River is mind boggling. These springs are the river's life source, and the river is the product of these springs.

Similarly, the *heart* is like a spring. It is our *life source* that feeds and fuels our existence. The Bible describes the heart as "the wellspring of life" and instructs us to "*guard it* above all else" (see Proverbs 4:23). The Encarta Dictionary says the heart is "the source and center of emotional life, where the deepest and sincerest feelings are located and a person is most vulnerable to pain."

Indeed, the heart is the fountain of our feelings and the root source of all our thoughts and actions. This is not only true of us, but also our children. Knowing your child's heart is the key to knowing what makes them tick and how to teach and train them in the right way.

> *Knowing your child's heart is the key to knowing what makes them tick and how to teach and train them in the right way.*

THE HEART MOTIVATES AND DIRECTS

Not only is the heart the wellspring of life, it is also the motivating force that propels your child in a specific direction. Like the motor on a boat, your child's heart sets the course in which he is headed and helps determine the speed at which he travels. It motivates what he *does*, what he *says*, how he *thinks*, and what he *feels*.

Our family has enjoyed going to the lake and watching many different types of boats. There are large yachts, medium-sized ski boats, and small jet skis. Interestingly, each is powered by one of two basic motors: an inboard motor or an outboard motor. While inboard motors are located inside the boat and covered by a protective hood or housing, outboard motors are attached to the outside of the boat and are easily seen.

Regardless of the type of boat, the motor (and attached rudder) helps controls two key things: the boat's speed and the direction it is going. Without a motor, the boat cannot travel or be pointed in a specific direction. It can be breathtakingly beautiful, having exquisite graphics on its sides and all the latest hi-tech bells and whistles available. But if it doesn't have a good motor, it is basically useless.

This is a good picture of your child's heart. Again, listen to the words of Proverbs 4:23—this time in the New Living Translation: "Guard your heart above all else, for *it determines the course of your life.*" Like a motor, your child's heart will guide him in a certain direction and determine how fast he gets there. He (or she) may be smart, popular, and good-looking on the outside, but if their heart is not pointed in the right direction, they're going to have recurring problems.

> *Like a motor, your child's heart will guide him in a certain direction and determine how fast he gets there.*

KNOW YOUR CHILD'S HEART

As a parent, it is vital for you to know and understand your child's heart. So many parents tend to focus on and deal with their kids' outward behavior, and they miss the real motivating force guiding their thoughts and actions. It's their "motor," or heart, that needs to be focused on and addressed.

Some children have a heart like an *outboard* motor. Everything about them is exposed and very visible, and it's easy to determine what is driving them. They wear their emotions (or heart) on their sleeve, freely and openly verbalizing their thoughts and feelings.

Other children have a heart like an *inboard* motor. In order to see what is driving them, you have to get underneath their hood. Their thoughts and feelings are hidden deep within, so to understand them, it takes some careful, patient probing.

If your child is like an "outboard," what is in their heart will be pretty obvious. If he is like an "inboard," you will really need to become a good listener. I have found that one of the best ways to determine what's in children's hearts is to listen to what's coming out of their mouths. Jesus said, "…For out of the overflow of the *heart* the mouth speaks" (Matthew 12:34). In other words, what is filling your child's heart will also fill their talk. All you have to do is open your ears and listen.

Knowing what kind of heart your child has will help you connect with and understand them. As a result, you will be empowered to teach and train them properly. By knowing their heart, you will know what is motivating and directing their life. If what is in their heart is harmful or unhealthy, you will know a course adjustment is needed. If it is wholesome and godly, you can heartily praise and encourage them to keep on keeping on.

One of the best ways to determine
what's in your child's heart is
to listen to what's coming out of his mouth.

GIVE APPROPRIATE INSTRUCTION AND DISCIPLINE

Once you have an accurate "pulse" on your child's heartbeat, you can begin giving appropriate instruction and discipline. This is critical to shaping their character and developing a trustworthy relationship. Looking back on my parenting days, there were times when it was vital for me to know that my children were telling me the truth.

Should I let them go to that place with this particular group of friends? I wondered. *Should I believe their explanation as to why they are late, or should I ground them for breaking curfew?*

Have you been there? Are you there now? Parents often wrestle with questions like these when it comes to raising children. In these challenging moments, it is imperative that you know your child's heart and can trust that he or she is telling the truth. Knowing their heart will help you discern the answers to these questions and decide whether the situation calls for instruction, discipline, or trust.

Not knowing your child's heart will increase the likelihood of making wrong assumptions regarding their motives. This can be very devastating. As a counselor, I have seen parents in situations like these. Some of them tend to lean toward the extreme of always believing their child is innocent. Sadly, in these cases, the parents are often the last to know that their child is in trouble. They are traumatized to discover their son is hooked on drugs. They are shocked when their daughter announces her pregnancy. They are horrified to learn that their teen has become a shooter at his school.

The parents of Eric Harris and Dylan Klebold, the students who carried out the Columbine High School massacre, are a perfect example. "Parents Blindsided by Plot" read the headline from the Denver Post.[2] They never suspected their sons of plotting such hideous deeds. Yet the boys did plot them and carry them out.

The other extreme I have seen parents who don't know their child's heart go to is to never trust their kids at all. *Let's play it safe,* they think. Out of fear of being deceived, they become extremely suspicious of their children. They never take them at their word and always believe the worst of their motives. The consequences of this practice can also be devastating.

For instance, suppose your child truly desires to do the right things. His heart strives for excellence. He works hard throughout his high school years and then announces that he wants to attend a four-year university across the state. Because you don't want to "be deceived," you tell him, "You can't go. All college kids drink and have sex, and you won't be any different."

What do you think a response like this will do to his heart? More than likely, it will crush him. In fact, if you could hear his heart speak, it would probably say, "What's the use of trying to do well? My parents don't believe in me. No one believes in me. I'll never amount to anything. If I'm being accused of wrong behavior, why shouldn't I just go ahead and do it?"

Friend, don't make wrong assumptions regarding your child's motives or parent them out of fear. Spend time with them and get to know their heart. Then you can give appropriate instruction and discipline when it's needed. At each age and stage of life, you can bring the course adjustments necessary to point them in the right direction and build in them a trustworthy character. By teaching and training their heart, you can put them in position to be the best they can possibly be.

By knowing your child's heart you can give appropriate instruction and discipline when it's needed.

CROSSING THE RIVER ON LADY
The Importance of Perseverance and Instilling Confidence in Your Children

When it comes to the importance of the heart, I am reminded of a situation that happened with our daughter, Stephanie. When she was five years old, we bought her a beautiful white pony. We named her *Lady*. Lady was the kind of pony everyone adored. She was just the right size for most children to ride and very well trained.

Now she didn't start out that way. In fact, when we first got her, her name wasn't even Lady—it was *Oscar*. Why Oscar, we are not sure. But after examining her private parts, we assumed that one of two things must have occurred. Either the previous owners had not cared to survey her anatomy and just guessed *she* was a *he*, or they named her after the Sesame Street character Oscar the Grouch. After several weeks of coming to her stall daily and attempting to love on her, we sided with option B.

Like a lot of children, Lady did not want to be trained. It took much coaxing and persistence on our part to convince her that doing what she was told would be in her best interest. She also seemed to care less about our daughter Stephanie. Every day our little girl talked to her, groomed her, and hugged her neck. But Lady paid her little attention. The only thing that little pony adored and lived for was *food*. That was her heart's motivation. The moment she heard grain rattling in a can or saw the movement of a person heading towards the hay, she came running.

She had the appetite of a supersonic vacuum cleaner. On trail rides, she would suck up our peanut butter and jelly sandwiches and fried chicken before we had the chance to stop her. "Don't be silly," we'd say. "Horses don't eat those things." But Lady was not your average horse.

We played a game with Stephanie and our son Alan when they rode Lady. If they could keep her head from diving down to inhale the grass while riding, they would get points. But if Lady caught them not paying attention, she would simply stop dead in her tracks and commence eating. While most horses and herd animals never want to be far from the pack, Lady had little or no desire to stay close with the others as they journeyed down the trail. It was all about food.

Well, when Stephanie was six, we took her and Lady with us on a week-long ride. Every day we rode over beautiful hills and crossed the river, always returning to the same campsite. One evening we experienced a deluge of rain. When we arrived at the river the next morning, it was slightly swollen, but we knew the river well and found a safe place to cross.

After riding for quite some time, we came out of the woods and saw that the river had risen since the morning. The normal path was now deeper, and the water was moving more swiftly. Since Lady's legs were quite a bit shorter than our horse's legs, the water would come up much higher on her body. If we crossed at the usual place, she would probably have to swim, and we didn't want to take that chance with Stephanie on board. Sending a taller horse out to make sure it would be safe for Lady to cross was the key to assessing a safer passage.

As we were studying the situation, so was Lady. Somehow her little horse brain realized that camp—aka food—was close at hand. She could see the green grass across the river, and just past that was the road that would take her straight to her food bin. With her eyes fixed on the prize, Lady jumped into the river before we could stop her. Immediately, she began swimming with Stephanie holding on for dear life. Unfortunately, the place she chose to jump in was not a good one. The swift current quickly began taking her and Stephanie downstream into waters that were over their heads. Terrified, we watched our daughter in peril, feeling helpless to rescue her.

After a quick calculation, we realized that there was no way we could reach her in time to pull her out. Lady's fat little body was being carried downstream fast, despite her effort to keep swimming. By now, Stephanie realized she was in trouble and began crying and screaming. This only made matters worse. When a person is crying or screaming, they are not thinking about what they need to do to get out of trouble. Instead, they are paralyzed by fear and/or pain, rendering themselves helpless. Of course, we did not blame Stephanie for her reaction, but somehow we needed to get her to calm down and refocus on getting to shore. She was the only one who could get herself out of danger.

Immediately, I prayed asking God for help and asking Him to enable Steph to tune into my voice and do what I would tell her to do. With all the strength I had, I yelled out with confidence (and anger at Lady), "Steph, you have a job to do. You can cry later, but right now you have to keep your eyes focused on the bank of the river directly ahead of you. You need to kick Lady as hard as you can and get her across!"

Upon hearing my confidence in her, she stopped crying, grabbed the reins, and proceeded to kick Lady as hard as she could. Miraculously, she made it to the other side! As soon as Lady got up on the river bank, she bent down and proceeded to graze. With a quick jerk, Stephanie yanked hard on the reins and yelled, "Oh, no you don't!"

As a parent, there will be times when your kids are in deep, troubled waters. Innately, you will want to jump in and save them, but they will be out of your reach. In those moments, the only thing you can do is pray and yell from the sidelines. By God's grace, you have gotten to know their heart and have taught them to listen to and obey your voice.

Our daughter experienced a perilous predicament that could have ended terribly. Somewhere underneath her panic lay the inner strength that could guide her heart out of fear and into faith and power. I needed to tap into that strength in a way I had never done before. To bring her to safety, I had to reach deep into her heart to pull out confidence in her own ability that I knew she had, but had forgotten. And I had to do it quickly so she could get where she needed to go!

After the ordeal was over, we used it as a life lesson. The lesson was that when you are in a crisis, you don't have time to cry. You just need to get through it, and when it is over, you can cry all you want. What a great lesson for Stephanie to learn. It certainly wasn't the way we would have chosen. However, it is a lesson that she has taken with her throughout her life. She has taught it to her riding students, used it in speeches, and applied it in personal times of crisis. What lesson did her father and I learn? Be leery of fat little ponies when the grass is greener on the other side!

Endnotes

[1] Quotes on the *Heart* (www.quotegarden.com/heart.html, accessed 9/20/13).

[2] "Parents Blindsided by Plot," by Mark Obmascik, Kevin Simpson, and Stacie Oulton (http://extras. denverpost.com/news/col1122.htm, accessed 9/20/13).

Reflection and Application

1. What would you say your child's heart is more like—an *outboard* or an *inboard* motor? What evidence in his or her life confirms this? How does this analogy help you better understand them?

    _____

    _____

    _____

2. Becoming a good listener is one of the best ways to hear and learn your child's heart. Their words paint a picture of what is inside them. Stop and think. What kind of things does your child talk about that produces...

    Joy and Excitement _____

    _____

    _____

    Peace and Contentment _____

    _____

    _____

    Confidence and Purpose _____

    _____

    _____

    This same exercise can be done with emotions like worry and fear, anger and rage, sadness and boredom. Knowing what brings out these emotions in your child will help you understand their likes and dislikes and know their heart.

3. After reading this chapter, are there any adjustments you feel prompted to make in the way you are relating to your child (or children)? If so, what are they? How can you better understand their heart?

    _____

    _____

    _____

"Rules without relationship leads to rebellion."

—**Josh McDowell**[1]

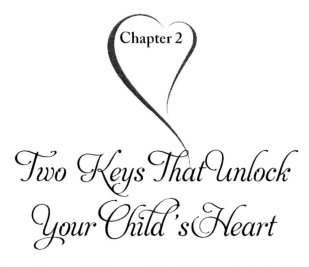

Chapter 2

Two Keys That Unlock Your Child's Heart

*"He will turn the hearts of the fathers to their children,
and the hearts of the children to their fathers...."*
Malachi 4:6

When it comes to parenting, there is a formula that I believe is very sound and deserves our attention. It involves three Rs and can be written one of two ways. The first way is:

Rules – Relationship = Rebellion

The second equation is similar to the first and just as important. It is:

Relationship – Rules = Rebellion

Rules without relationship will lead to rebellion. Likewise, having a relationship with your kids without having any rules will prove to be just as devastating. A balance of the two is needed to help produce happy, healthy children who can stand on their own two feet and be a blessing to the world around them. Relationship and rules are two master keys that unlock your child's heart.

> *Relationship and rules are two master keys that unlock your child's heart.*

THE VALUE OF RELATIONSHIP

In the real estate world, there is a saying that defines the three most valuable aspects of a piece of property: "It's about location, location, location." Similarly, when it comes to raising our children, "It's about *relationship, relationship, relationship.*"

Without question, developing a relationship with your child is a major key to unlocking his or her heart. They will not listen to your instruction, pay attention to your discipline, or respect your authority if you do not have a relationship with them. To train them up in the way they should go, you must know their heart and understand who God made them to be. And this is accomplished through relationship.

One of the two extremes found frequently in childrearing are parents who major on rules and consequences and don't take the time to cultivate a relationship with their kids. Many times, those who have this tendency are those who lived a rebellious life as a teen. They know firsthand the possible outcome of leading an undisciplined life and are determined that their kids will not repeat it. In their attempt to protect, they become very rule oriented and strict in their parenting, often with lasting negative effects.

Teens growing up in this atmosphere often feel they are paying for the "sins of their father."[2] Even though they did not grow up in the same environment as their mom and dad and were actually taught right from wrong, their parents expect them to behave the same way they did. Suspicion and a lack of trust shroud the children like a black cloud, causing them to feel smothered and condemned without cause. The word "no" becomes a standard response. And even kids who start out with a desire to do right often end up rebelling in their teen years.

Rule-driven parenting is like a dead-end road. Children will often listen and even comply with instructions, but in their hearts they grow more and more distant from their parents. As I said, they often rebel and end up going off the deep end into various destructive behaviors. But even in cases when they don't, their hearts become angry and bitter. They long for the day they can leave and get out from under their parent's authority. Yes, rules are needed, but not in the absence of relationship. What children need first and foremost is a relationship based in love.

Your children will not listen to instruction, pay attention to your discipline, or respect your authority if you do not have a relationship with them.

THE FOUNDATION OF YOUR RELATION IS UNCONDITIONAL LOVE

Building a solid relationship with your children must include *unconditional love*. It is both the foundation and the glue that holds you together. The greatest need of every human being is to be loved and accepted. The moment your children were born, they unconsciously began to crave love. Throughout each age and stage of their life—from a kindergartner going to school for the first time to a college student making new friends on campus—they will seek love and acceptance from others. But the love and acceptance offered is almost always conditional.

Conditional love is earned and requires an exchange; it says, "If you do this, then I will do that." Our behavior, thoughts, and opinions are the standard that others examine and critique (often in unspoken terms). From this they determine whether to give us love and acceptance. With few exceptions, conditional love is the kind of love the world has to offer your children.

Take "little Johnny," for example. He has counted the days until he goes to school for the first time, and he is very excited. He finally gets to be a "big boy" and meet new friends, play games, and go to recess. He has a new back pack, new school clothes, and a broad smile as he proudly marches off to school. However, when he gets there, one of his "new friends" immediately attacks him, calling him names he's never been called before. He is shocked and confused as to why he is being talked to that way. The words dig quickly into his soul. Tears run down his face as some of the other kids join in to make fun of the "cry baby." His joy is crushed, and he begins to believe, perhaps for the first time, that there is something wrong with him.

Then there is "Kate," the junior high girl who discovers that school life revolves around a popularity contest. It seems that education is simply a side note. Every day she is judged by the clothes she wears, the style of her hair and makeup, and whether or not she has blemishes. What she says, what she doesn't say, who she hangs out with, who she doesn't hang out with, and what morals she has or pretends to have are also up for scrutiny. Sending her to school and telling her to have a good day is like sending a lamb into a pack of wolves alone.

When Kate and Johnny return, open the door and say, "I'm home," they need to feel they are loved—no matter what they did or didn't do, said or didn't say, wore or didn't wear, blemishes and all. Home should be the safest place on earth. Why? Because it is filled with unconditional love. They are free to express their thoughts and feelings as long as they do so respectfully.

When you unconditionally love your kids, you are basically saying, "I love you *no matter what you do*! I may not agree with all your behavior and opinions, but I always love you." This kind of love is not natural. It cannot be bought in a store or acquired through education. Unconditional love can only be received through a relationship with Jesus Christ.

> *For a healthy relationship, your kids need unconditional love. It cannot be bought or acquired through education. It can only be received through a relationship with Jesus.*

Scripture says, "For God so *loved* the world that He gave His one and only Son, that whoever believes in him shall not perish but have eternal life" (John 3:16). Unconditional love is the kind of love Christ has for us. No matter what we do, whether we are saved or unsaved, His love for us remains the same. However, when we admit that we are sinners, ask God for His forgiveness, and invite Jesus to come live in us, we are *given the divine ability* to unconditionally love others—including our children.

As a son or daughter of God, Christ loves you. His love is not based on what you achieve, think, or feel. His love is based totally on Him. Like any good father, there are times when God will warn, correct, and instruct you. Nevertheless, He loves you—even

41

when you mess up and are mean and nasty to others. And the best news is, "…there is nothing in all creation that will ever be able to separate us from the love of God which is ours through Christ Jesus our Lord" (Romans 8:39 GNT).

If you are in relationship with God through Jesus, His Son, you are loved and you have the ability to unconditionally love your children. Romans 5:5 reveals that "…God has poured out his love into our hearts by the Holy Spirit, whom he has given us." How can you tap into the love of God that has been poured into your heart? Simply ask Him for it in prayer. Say, "Lord, help me to love my children unconditionally and build a good relationship with them. You said You have poured Your love into my heart, and I need that love to love my kids. Please help me." God will hear and answer your prayer, and He will begin to help you love your children like never before!

YOUR KIDS *WANT* A GOOD RELATIONSHIP

Believe it or not, most children—including teens—want to have a good relationship with their parents! Now, you may be reading this and thinking, *No way! You don't know my kid. He barely says a word to me. Just about every time I suggest doing something together, he rolls his eyes at me. The last thing he wants is a relationship!* Well, that may be his reaction on the outside and the façade he wants you to see. However, underneath that rough exterior is most likely a child yearning for your love and acceptance.

The truth is, hurt is often masked and expressed as anger or an "I don't care" attitude. In my practice, I have observed kids drop their tough act once they get in touch with what's inside their heart. Once they express their hurt over mom and dad not taking the time to develop a relationship with them, their demeanor changes.

To me, some children are a lot like M & Ms. They have a colorful, hardened shell on the outside that protects a soft, sweet core on the inside. Think about it. What baby or toddler did not begin life craving the love and acceptance of their mommy and daddy? Their nourishment, security, and very existence rested in the loving arms and smooches of their parents.

What happens to their desire for a loving relationship? It becomes muddled as they grow. Negative experiences along with weaknesses in personalities are contributing factors. Add to this the menacing effects of peer pressure. It says things like, "It's not cool to have a relationship with your parents. Talking with them and participating in family outings is embarrassing."

Of course, we know this isn't true. But the teen years can be a confusing time to navigate for both parents and teens. Young people have been hurled into the "world of in-between"—torn between the desire to remain a child and a longing to become an adult. They are no longer children, yet not quite ready for adulthood. If we treat them as a child, they can become defensive because they don't feel trusted. If we treat them as an adult, the responsibility may be too great, and the world becomes a fearful place to live.

What is the answer? How can you prepare yourself and your children for this critical time in their lives and maintain the good relationship you both want? I believe it all goes back to taking the time to know their heart and having a relationship with God. He will help you stay involved in your kids' lives and keep you connected with them in relationship. Within this healthy environment, they are ready and more willing to hear and receive your rules.

> *Believe it or not, most children want to have a good relationship with their parents. Underneath their rough exterior is a child yearning for your love and acceptance.*

THE NEED FOR RULES

Along with relationship, there must be *rules*. Rules provide structure and discipline in the home and help children feel safe and secure in their environment. A life without rules is a disaster waiting to happen.

Throughout my counseling practice, I have encountered a number of parents whose number one goal in raising their children is to find a way to get along with them. They want to be their child's *best friend*. Once this goal is accomplished, they breathe a sigh of relief and begin the next task of defending their child's choices—specifically choices that are unwise and unhealthy.

For these parents, it is all about having a relationship. Rules in the household are viewed as unnecessary and only seem to interfere. They feel their child will learn on their own and "find their own way." But experience has proven that this philosophy is flawed. As the Bible says, "To discipline a child produces wisdom, but a mother is disgraced by an undisciplined child" (Proverbs 29:15 NLT).

As shocking as it may seem, I have had parents tell me that they smoke pot with their pre-teen because "they are going to do it anyway." They are willing to allow their child to do something they know in their heart is unhealthy in an effort to maintain their "best-friend" status. The majority of these parents hate conflict, so they avoid it like a plague.

For instance, it is difficult for them to confront their ten year old when he refuses to clean out the litter box or tell their four-teen year old that he cannot sleep at a friend's house on a school night. To them, confronting their child will negatively impact their relationship. And so rather than address the child's rebellion and disobedience, it becomes easier for them to clean the litter box themselves and let their child spend the night with his friend. Eventually, this pattern of parenting often becomes detrimental to the child's wellbeing.

> *Establishing and enforcing rules that your kids know will be here today as well as tomorrow are the guardrails to keep them traveling safely down the highway of life.*

At one point in my life, I worked at a detention center, and one of my duties was to supervise inmate visits with their parents. Several came religiously every week to visit their sons. Often-times I overheard many of them blaming the police, the judge, their lawyer, and even the victim for their precious fair-haired boy being in jail. Interestingly, these parents were the ones we had to carefully scan because of their attempts to sneak in contraband.

In keeping with their mindset to be their child's buddy, these parents were usually quick to provide their son with cigarettes and any other commissary needs he had. They also provided bond money to secure his release, no matter the cost. Eventually, he would get out of jail. And although he would swear he had been unjustly accused, it would only be a matter of months before he returned for another crime.

If you tend to gravitate toward being your child's best friend at all costs, please hear my heart. In the absence of rules, your child will eventually rebel. Yes, having a good relationship is vital, but so are rules. He or she needs clearly defined structure in their life, and that is what rules provide. No, they probably won't like it, but deep in their heart they want it. In the years ahead, they will realize the tremendous value of rules and thank you for them.

Establishing and enforcing rules that your kids know will be here today as well as tomorrow are the *guardrails* to keep them traveling safely down the highway of life. They can rest assured that not only will consequences follow disobedience, but rewards will follow when they choose to obey. Is it any wonder the prophet Isaiah declared, "Oh Lord, your discipline is good and leads to life and health. Oh, heal me and make me live!" (Isaiah 38:16 TLB) Helping your children understand the importance of obedience will serve them well their entire life.

RELATIONSHIP PLUS RULES IS THE KEY!

I would like to propose one additional formula: R + R = I. That is, *relationship* plus *rules* equal a passport to *instruct*. As you take the time to develop a good relationship with your child and establish good rules that you consistently enforce, your instruction will now be listened to and hopefully, embedded in their heart. A healthy balance of relationship and rules creates an environment in which they will respect what you are teaching them.

Proverbs 1:8-9 states, "Listen, my son, to your father's *instruction* and do not forsake your mother's teaching. They will be a garland to grace your head and a chain to adorn your neck." If you want your child to embrace your instruction, he or she must be hearing it from someone they know loves them unconditionally and is not afraid to apply discipline.

Again, to train up your children in the way they should go, you need to develop both a healthy relationship and establish life-giving rules you consistently enforce. This creates the environment for them to hear and receive instruction.

> *A healthy balance of relationship and rules creates an environment in which your children will respect and receive your instruction.*

In the chapters ahead, we will talk more about instruction as well as explore three major building blocks of a good relationship and learn how the value of rules can last for a lifetime. But first, we will take a look at four basic styles of parenting.

Endnotes

[1] Quotes by *Josh McDowell* (www.goodreads.com/author/quotes/ 4314.Josh_McDowell, accessed 9/21/13).

[2] See Exodus 20:1-6; Deuteronomy 24:16.

Reflection and Application

1. Having a *relationship* with your child is a major key to unlocking their heart. Stop and think. How would you describe the condition of your relationship with them? Is it vibrant, mediocre, or nonexistent? Does your love tend to be conditional or unconditional? What evidence confirms this condition?

   _____

   _____

   _____

2. What practical things can you do to improve the level of your relationship with your child (or children)? Likewise, what adjustments can you make personally and in your home to help them feel unconditionally loved?

   _____

   _____

   _____

For questions 1 and 2, take a few moments to pray. Get God involved by asking Him for wisdom to see the things you need to see and do what you can to bring about positive change.

3. *Rules* are a second major key to unlocking your child's heart. Again, stop and think. What are the **top ten** rules in your home? Do your children know them? Take a few moments and write them down. Then schedule a time you can share them with your kid(s) in a non-threatening atmosphere.

   _____

   _____

   _____

*As you develop your **top ten**, think about the most important principles you want your kids to know and take with them when they leave home. Yes, other rules may be needed, but your **top ten** are the most important and serve as a foundation for the rest.*

"When our children were growing up, we said two things to them over and over again: 'Obey God' and 'Always do your best.' These two things served as the basis of what we considered excellence in our home. …I highly recommend that parents adopt these two standards for raising their children because character development is clearly emphasized over performance."

—**Charles Stanley**[1]

The Four Basic Styles of Parenting

"And now a word to you parents. Don't keep on scolding
and nagging your children, making them angry and resentful.
Rather, bring them up with the loving discipline the Lord himself
approves, with suggestions and godly advice."
Ephesians 6:4 TLB

There are four basic styles of parenting that I see most often in my practice. As we learned in the last chapter, some parents major on just the rules, while abandoning the relationship. For others, it is all about relationship and nothing about rules. Then there is a third parent who is a combination of all the wrong qualities and a fourth parent who is a balance of the right qualities.

Again, good parenting requires a *balance* of relationship and rules. It is a healthy combination of both love and justice. These qualities create the optimum environment for children to hear and receive instruction and to grow. As I describe each of these different styles, you will probably see yourself in one or more of them. And that's okay; don't be alarmed or discouraged. Being able to identify your parenting style will help you see the areas in which you are most challenged and where you need to make adjustments. Are you ready? Then let's begin.

Good parenting requires a balance of relationship and rules. It is a healthy combination of both love and justice.

THE "P" OR PERMISSIVE PARENT

The first style of parenting is the "P" or *Permissive* parent. The Permissive parent has *high* levels of love and *low* levels of justice. They want to be their child's best friend. You know, the "cool" parent who is liked by all the kids and considered to be "one of us." Sadly, in their attempts to be friends with their children, they seldom say "no." Hence the name *permissive*. They are lenient, lackadaisical, laidback, and tolerant of their kids. Heaven forbid if they do or say something to make their child upset.

These people hate conflict and certainly don't want it with their children. They will rationalize and give reasons for their child's inappropriate behavior with statements such as, "Boys will be boys," and "It's just a phase they are going through. They'll grow out of it." I have seen children climb on their friend's furniture and jump up and down on their couches while their parents were in the same room conversing. Shockingly, the parents are oblivious to it. Do they really not see what their child is doing? Or do they expect others to simply tolerate their child's behavior as though it is to be expected?

When they do say "no" to their child, they try to persuade him or her to go along with them. But ultimately, the child ends up making the decision. In fact, they basically create their own rules for governing their lives. The results are often devastating.

The most common byproduct of Permissive parenting is children who lack self-discipline. For instance they fail to make good grades on their tests because they "didn't feel like studying." They are often late for school because they missed the bus; they were too tired and "didn't feel like getting up." Permissive parents are the ones who usually show up at school to defend their precious child because the teachers and administrators are just too hard on them. After all, their child is a "victim" of a bad administration.

As their child grows, the "P" parent continues to deny or excuse their inappropriate behavior, which is now evident to all. Once they reach their teenage and adult years, they struggle to stay employed. Some are fired because they were supposed to be at work by 8:00 a.m., but they just didn't see why they couldn't arrive at 8:15 a.m. Lacking vital boundaries in their lives, these kids are easily swayed to make choices that are detrimental to their wellbeing. What's more, they tend to lack responsibility and become "blamers." "It's the police's fault that I'm in jail," they declare to mom and dad who in turn echo the same sentiment while paying their child's bail. In these kids' minds, the reason they are in the situation they are in has to be someone else's fault.

The Permissive parent has high levels of love and low levels of justice. They tend to raise children who lack self-discipline.

The Bible gives us examples of children whose parents were permissive. Take for instance Eli the priest. He had two sons, Hophni and Phinehas, who were extremely disobedient and offensive to God and others. The Scripture says Eli knew about the wrong things his sons were doing, but "…he failed to restrain them" (1 Samuel 3:13). As a result, God Himself had to discipline them and their lives were cut short.[2]

A similar situation happened with King David. Two of his sons, Absalom and Adonijah, were very handsome and destined for greatness. However, they both had character flaws that David never addressed. Speaking of Adonijah, the Bible says, "Now his father, King David, had *never disciplined him at any time*, even by asking, 'Why are you doing that?'…" (1 Kings 1:6 NLT). Sadly, like Eli's sons, both Absalom and Adonijah's lives were cut short, and they were outlived by their father.

Friend, if you have the tendencies of a Permissive parent, please take notice of these examples. Don't beat yourself up or feel like a failure. Simply ask God for help to make the changes you need to make to bring appropriate discipline to your children. Remember, "A refusal to correct is a refusal to love; love your children by disciplining them" (Proverbs 13:24 The Message).

The "L" or Legalistic

On the other side of that spectrum is the "L" or *Legalistic* parent. While the Permissive parent has high levels of love and low levels of justice, the Legalistic parent has *low* levels of love and *high* levels of justice. They place little value on relationships and love. It is all about the rules, which are set in stone and had better be followed. These parents rule with an iron fist, creating an atmosphere of fear and anxiety in which the child lives. Legalistic parents tend to look at life through a black and white lens. Seldom are there any gray areas. Consequently, virtually everything is viewed as having a right or a wrong way, and the parent defines which is which.

Unlike Permissive parents, Legalistic parents welcome conflict. Arguing with them is like debating a prosecuting attorney. They will either explain relentlessly why something will be done a certain way or answer with a curt, "Because I said so."

> *The Legalistic parent has low levels of love and high levels of justice. They place little value on relationships. It's all about the rules.*

Sometimes, the Legalistic parent's motivation to be the way they are is based on their own fear. They do not want their children to go through the same things they experienced, so they create high expectations and attempt to put "the fear of God" into them so they won't fail. Other "L" parents are motivated by a need for safety and security. They feel that if everyone thinks the same way they do, including their children, their world is secure.

All in all, children of "L" homes tend to feel like a failure. Again and again, they struggle and strain to win their parent's acceptance, but in most cases fail to achieve it. Like all children, they desire to feel loved and valued for who they are. But love is based on their performance, or works. It is not the unconditional love they desperately need. If they don't "make the grade," they don't get the love.

Some children who grow up under Legalistic parents continue trying to please them throughout their adult years. Others turn away from their parents and their parent's values out of anger or despair. They determine that they will never measure up, so why even try. Interestingly, some children from "L" homes grow up and struggle in the same areas as those from the "P" homes. They become rebellious and often make bad choices that negatively impact their lives. Tired of hearing how they don't measure up, they too become blamers and justify that their actions are not their fault.

The Legalistic parent seldom says, "I love you," or shows up at their child's activities. Because these children are not rewarded for a job well done and nothing really changes in their lives, they simply give up trying to be good. Indifference becomes the norm. In some cases, personality disorders arise from this style of parenting—specifically schizophrenia.

The best direction I can provide for this style of parenting is the word of instruction found in Ephesians 6:4. "And now a word to you parents. Don't keep on scolding and nagging your children, making them angry and resentful. Rather, bring them up with the loving discipline the Lord himself approves, with suggestions and godly advice" (TLB). Again, *balance* is the key. Yes, children need discipline, but it must be done lovingly and in the setting of a healthy relationship.

In the words of the great Martin Luther, "Spare the rod and spoil the child—that is true. But, beside the rod, keep an apple to give him when he has done well."[3]

"Spare the rod and spoil the child—that is true. But, beside the rod, keep an apple to give him when he has done well." —**Martin Luther**[4]

The "M" or Manipulated Parent

The next parenting style is quickly becoming more common in our society. It is the "M" or *Manipulated* parent. This style combines *low* levels of love and *low* levels of justice. Parents adopting this pattern suffer from a lack of effort either because of time restraints or they have other more important interests besides parenting. One of the best ways I know to describe an "M" parent is to share a typical conversation between them and their child. It would sound something like this:

Child: "Can I go to the movies tonight?"

M Parent: "No, it's a school night."

Child: "But, why not? Everyone else is going."

M Parent: "You'll get home too late."

Child: "No I won't. I want to go! Come on, I really need to go. All my friends are going to be there."

M Parent: (voice raised) "Why can't you go on the weekend?"

Child: (whiney and frustrated) "Because they're all going tonight, not this weekend. Come on..."

The battle continues until the "M" parent gives in and the child hops merrily off to the movies. Communication between this parent and their child becomes a game. Both players know that the "M" parent's first response will not be taken seriously. They also have an unspoken rule: "My parent's answers do not mean anything. Their 'no' does not mean 'no.' I just need to wear them down and keep driving my point, and they will give in to my desires."

Now, it is normal for all children to question authority and push the limits to see what will happen. Most toddlers will cry when they don't get their way. But if a child gets what he or she wants when they cry, they will quickly learn to use that cry to see if it works again. That's what the child of an "M" parent does. They are able to see this unspoken rule as early as age three and manipulate their parents into getting whatever they want.

Have you ever seen this scenario play out at a store or mall? You hear the child ask his "M" parent if he can have a toy on the shelf. The parent says "no." At that, the child either begins to debate with the parent or cry and carry on. This continues until the parent frustratingly says, "Fine. You can have the toy. Just quit crying." This is a picture of an "M" parent's unspoken rule in action.

If the child would have said, "Okay, Mom," and had given up the opportunity to battle, the "M" parent would have gone into shock! Again, the child knows the rule. "If I continue pursuing what I want, I will get it."

> *The Manipulated parent has low levels of love and low levels of justice. They suffer from a lack of effort because of time restraints or they have other interests besides parenting.*

Unfortunately, we have a lot of "M" parents in our society today. Many parents work outside the home and are exhausted when they walk in the front door. Immediately, they are met with the demands for dinner, piles of laundry, and arguing children. They just don't want to engage in a battle. Many know what is right and what they need to do, but they just don't want to be bothered.

The typical product of an "M" parent home is the same as that of a "P" parent home—children who lack self-discipline. Any child who insists on getting his way and then gets it will likely lack the understanding of responsibility. As adults, they tend to feel like a victim when the rest of society doesn't give in to their demands.

If you find yourself exhibiting the Manipulated parent tendencies, your situation is not hopeless. There *is* time to make some changes. You may be exhausted and have little or no desire to build a relationship with your children or give them the appropriate discipline they need. If this is you, be honest and tell God how you feel. If you ask Him for help, He will give it!

In Isaiah 40:29-31, God says that "He gives power to the weak and strength to the powerless. Even youths will become weak and tired, and young men will fall in exhaustion. But those who trust in the Lord will find *new strength*..." (NLT).

And in Psalm 37:4, He says that as you "delight yourself also in the Lord...He shall give you the *desires* of your heart" (NKJV). If you are fed up with having low levels of love and low levels of justice in your home, open the door and invite God in! He cares about you and your kids more than you will ever know. He will empower you to be the godly parent you want to be.

Are you fed up with having low levels of love and low levels of justice in your home? Open the door and invite God in! He cares about you and your kids more than you know.

THE "G" OR GODLY PARENT

The fourth style of parenting is the "G" or Godly parent. This is a biblical style that requires *high* levels of love and *high* levels of justice. This parent is the one who says, "Honey, I love you too much to let you get by with that," and then they administer the appropriate discipline. They believe in *training* their child, not babysitting them. They will persist and endure even when they are tired. They are willing to discipline them consistently because they love them deeply and want what's best for them.

What does a high level of justice look like in a Godly style of parenting? Three words sum it up: *Loving, Consistent Discipline.* In order for your discipline to be effective, it must consistent and administered in an attitude of love. If a behavior was disciplined last week, it needs to be disciplined this week and the next. It does not matter if you are tired or busy; wrong attitudes and behavior must consistently be addressed in a loving way.

"But what am I supposed to do when I'm angry?" *Press pause* on the situation. If you are at home, send your child to their room and give yourself time to settle down. Promise them that they are going to be disciplined, but you will do it with a right, loving heart. As one Bible teacher eloquently stated, "Let your emotions subside and then decide what needs to be done."

If you discipline out of anger, your children will also become angry. God's Word says, "Human anger does *not* produce the righteousness God desires" (James 1:20 NLT). In other words, your angry outburst will not produce the right behavior your child needs. As a Godly parent, you must apply the principle of Ephesians 6:4 stated earlier. "Fathers, do not exasperate your children; instead, bring them up in the training and instruction of the Lord." Disciplining in anger will exasperate your children.

Disciplining in love will provide them instruction. Remember, your goal is to *train them*, not just raise them. As you keep this goal in sight, it will help you bring proper discipline.

Overall, Godly parenting is heavy on the relationship, consistent in the discipline, and insightful in the instruction. These parents are involved in their kids' lives, going to their baseball games and dance recitals—cheering them on in all their endeavors. If their boyfriend or girlfriend breaks up with them, they are there to comfort and hold them if needed. Incorporating this style of parenting says to your child, "I believe in you. I know God has a plan and a purpose for your life. You can be anything you want to be."

> *Godly parenting is heavy on the relationship,*
> *consistent on the discipline and*
> *insightful in the instruction.*

The result of Godly parenting is usually a peaceful household and peaceful children. Oh, there are conflicts, but they are dealt with promptly, properly, and prayerfully. God is the center of it all. Children of Godly parents have more freedom to go places because they know the rules and know that those rules will be enforced.

Of all the styles of parenting, Godly parenting should be your goal. It yields the highest and best results for both you and your children. Godly parenting produces godly children. And God says, "The father {*and mother*} of godly children has cause for joy. What a pleasure to have children who are wise" (Proverbs 23:24 NLT).

In the next section, we will focus on three vital building blocks of a good relationship: the need for *cultivation*, the power of *communication*, and the importance of *observation*. Now, take a few moments to reflect on this chapter and apply its principles to your own life.

Endnotes

[1]Charles Stanley, *How to Keep Your Kids on Your Team* (Nashville, TN: Oliver-Nelson Books, a division of Thomas Nelson, Inc., Publishers, 1986) p. 62.
[2]For the full story on Eli and his sons, check out 1 Samuel 2:12-36; 3:11-18; 4:10-18.
[3]Christian quotes on *Parenting* (www.dailychristianquote.com/dcqfamily.html#Children, accessed 9/24/13). (4) Ibid.

Reflection and Application

1. Of the four parenting styles—*Permissive, Legalistic, Manipulated,* and *Godly*—which style(s) best describes you? Why? What specific actions and attitudes confirm this?

    _____

    _____

    _____

2. Can you remember the home you grew up in? In light of this chapter and your childhood memories, what type of parenting style would you say best describes your parents? Considering how you turned out as an adult, what lesson(s) can you learn and apply in your own life as a parent?

    _____

    _____

    _____

    For questions 1 and 2, take a few moments to pray. Get God involved by asking Him for wisdom to see the things you need to see and remember what you need to remember. Ask Him to fill in the gaps your parents (or the absence of parents) left in your life and heart.

3. All of us have room for improvement as parents. Thankfully, God does not condemn us or love us less for the mistakes we have made. He stands ready, willing and able to help us overcome every poor parenting style we may be dealing with.

    Take a few moments to pause and pray. Here is sample prayer to consider:

    "Father God, You know all the things I experienced while growing up, and You know why I am the way I am and why I parent my kids the way I do. There are things that need to change, but only You can empower me to change them. Please help me. Show me specifically what I can do to be a godly parent, and help me trust You to do what I cannot do. In Jesus' name, Amen."

    _____

    _____

    _____

    Take time to be still and listen to what God speaks to your heart. Write down what He reveals. His words are priceless!

Part II:

The Building Blocks of a Good Relationship

"In raising children, every-thing depends on the love relationship between the parent and child. Nothing works well if a child's love needs are not met. Only the child who feels genuinely loved and cared for can do her best."

—**Gary Chapman and Ross Campbell**[1]

The Need for Cultivation

"Children are a gift from the Lord;
they are a reward from him."
Psalm 127:3 NLT

*H*opefully, it is becoming clear that having a relationship with your children is a major key to getting to their heart. And the first building block to your relationship is *cultivation*. Essentially, cultivation is taking the time to listen to, talk, and interact with your children. Your relationship with them is a lot like a garden. It requires planting good seeds, regular watering, and consistent, loving nurturing in order for it to grow and flourish.

BE INTENTIONAL WITH YOUR CHILDREN

Every child—regardless of gender, nationality, or age—spells love "T I M E." In his book, *Turning Hearts Towards Home*, Dr. James Dobson describes his relationship with his father. Due to a rigorous business schedule on the road, Dobson's dad made a deliberate effort to spend long hours with James while he was home. They fished, played tennis, and hunted together as often as possible. Dr. Dobson recalls his special memories of getting up early with his dad to walk in the woods and observe the beauty of the things God created.

Again and again, they conversed about life and spiritual matters. "But most importantly," Dobson recalls, "there was something dramatic that occurred between my dad and me out there in the forest. An intense love and affection was generated on those mornings that set the tone for a lifetime of fellowship. There was a closeness and a oneness that made me want to be like that man…. that made me choose his values as my values, his dreams as my dreams, his God as my God."[2]

What a powerful relationship that Dr. Dobson and his father had—so powerful that he desired his father's dreams, values, and his God. It is vital to note that James' father was *intentional* in cultivating a relationship with his son. It didn't just happen automatically. As a result, a special love and affection between them developed—an affection Dr. Dobson still treasures today.

> *Cultivation is taking the time to listen to, talk,*
> *and interact with your children.*

You might say, "That's all well and good, but, remember, I'm the one with the child who doesn't want anything to do with cultivating a relationship with me." Well, that may or may not be true. Remember, when our kids are hurt, they often throw up a smokescreen of bad behavior. But deep inside, they really want a relationship. That being said, don't let their words stop you from doing what you need to do as a parent. Be intentional—pursue cultivating a relationship on purpose.

Become a student of your child, discovering his or her greatest interests. Then regularly suggest doing an activity together that they like. If they seem resistant, don't give up. Your child is worth pursuing! Just as you are.

GOD IS INTENTIONAL WITH YOU

Think about this. God pursues us *on purpose*. He did not wait for us to seek Him first; He was the initiator of our relationship. Romans 5:8 confirms this, declaring, "…God demonstrates his own love for us in this: While we were still sinners, Christ died for us." Aren't you glad He didn't wait for us to recognize we were sinners and ask for His forgiveness before sending Jesus? I know I am!

God not only was the initiator of our relationship in the beginning, He continues to be the initiator even now. There are times in our lives when we don't feel like "hanging out" with Him. We may have ignored Him, disobeyed Him, or misrepresented Him and given Him a bad name. Yet, He still pursues us diligently and patiently and loves us whether we deserve it or not. His love is not based on our works or our desire to have a relationship with Him. It is not dictated by our mood or our level of maturity. His love and desire for relationship is based on Him and Him alone. God *is* love. It is not just something He does; it is who He is. And that will never change!

Romans 8:35, 38-39 describes how the Lord pursues us: "Who shall separate us from the love of Christ? Shall trouble or hardship or persecution or famine or nakedness or danger or sword? For I am convinced that neither death nor life, neither angels nor demons, neither the present nor the future, nor any powers, neither height nor depth, nor anything else in all creation, will be able to separate us from the love of God that is in Christ Jesus our Lord."

Wow! What an encouraging promise. And what a great example for us, as parents, to pursue that diligent relationship with our children. To put that verse in a parental pledge could look very similar:

"Who shall separate us from the love of our children? Shall trouble or hardship or persecution or drugs or homosexuality or hurtful statements made? For I, as their parent, am convinced, that neither death nor life, neither angels nor demons, nor anything else that they do—good or bad—will be able to separate me from the love I have for them because of the love of God that is in Christ Jesus."

Again, we love God because He *first* loved us (see 1 John 4:19). Your children desire this same unconditional love that you do. With His strength, you can love your children and pursue them as Christ loves and pursues you—even when they don't deserve it or think they need you.

God pursues us diligently and patiently
and loves us whether we deserve it or not.
His love and desire for relationship is
based on Him and Him alone. God is love.

WAYS TO SPEND *QUALITY* AND *QUANTITY* TIME TOGETHER

"Spending time with our children is about quality, not quantity." Have you heard this statement before? It is one that has been spouted many times in answer to the proverbial question of how much time parents should spend with their kids. It seems to be used most often by parents who maintain a very busy schedule and work long hours outside of the home. While quality time is very important, quantity also yields great value and is needed to adequately cultivate a good relationship.

Thankfully, there are ways to spend both quantity and quality time with your children, whether you have to work full time or not. Here are a few ideas to consider that have proven to be effective.

SHARE MEALS TOGETHER

Few places offer better bonding opportunities than time spent around the table. For thousands of years, mealtime has proven to be a powerful place for people to connect—especially parents and children. I know that this can be very challenging for many families with kids involved in school sports, scouting, and other activities. However, it is a great chance for all members of the family to reconnect at the same time.

Sharing meals together was a challenge for our family during certain seasons. Our son was involved in after-school sports, and our daughter was avidly teaching horse-riding lessons. There were many nights that our dinners did not take place until 8:00 or 9:00 p.m. There were also times that a sit-down, all-inclusive meal just did not work. But we adapted and made up for it in the days that followed. Participating in family dinners was not a rigid "rule" that we held over our kid's heads; it was just considered "what we do" as a family. If you have a family member whose schedule requires them to be late during a normal dinner hour, consider eating at a later time. Flexibility is the key.

There are a number of advantages to sharing meals together. Most importantly, it is a purposeful "time out" for each family member. Everyone steps off their treadmill of busyness to reconnect with others. It is a time of open communication—talking, listening, giving encouragement, and finding out what has been going on in each person's life.

To make the most of your mealtimes, here are a few suggestions. Start off each meal with prayer, thanking God for His faithful provision of food. You can also include requests for God's help in your prayers. Petitions like, "Lord, please help John with his test tomorrow. Be with Susie when she talks to Rachel; give her the words to say to mend their relationship." Prayer brings God into your family and unites each member on a deeper, spiritual level. It also expresses genuine love, care, and support to your children and helps connect them in relationship with God—the Parent of all parents.

The other piece of advice I want to give is to turn off the TV and all other electronic devices. Electronic intrusion suffocates relationships. As author and speaker Jimmy Evans so aptly put it, "Electronics make great servants, but they are terrible masters." Keep in mind that meals are about building relationships and enjoying good food. So turn off the TV, the iPad, your cell phone, etc., and just chill with your children. The return on your investment will be well worth it.

For thousands of years, mealtime has proven to be a powerful place for people to connect—especially parents and children.

HAVE FUN TOGETHER

As the old saying goes, "A family that plays together stays together." Indeed, having fun as a family infuses life-giving energy into your relationships. And children really are a lot of fun! Their innocent remarks and unique perspective on life can be quite humorous and insightful.

I remember a time when our daughter Stephanie was four. She found a dead bird in the yard and was really heartbroken over it. Sobbing, she came and asked what we should do with the bird. Hearing her concern, my husband, Don, suggested that they bury it. Together, they dug a small hole for the "casket" (an old shoe box) and we had a "funeral." Each of us spoke kind words, sharing how the bird probably had a good life and a nice family. We even made a little cross for the burial site. When the funeral concluded, I will never forget Stephanie's response. She said, "Hey dad that was fun! Let's kill another bird so we can do this again." Kids! They really do say the funniest things.

Games are great. Our family loves to play games—especially board games that are appealing to our children's personalities. We started this practice when they were three and four years old. We selected games that were fun and kept everyone on an equal playing field. Family game nights would always be accompanied by an array of "junk food" to make the evening extra special.

If you have not experienced the fun of playing games with your kids, it is never too late to start! Yes, they may seem reluctant or skeptical at first, but if you can get one child to play, the others will likely join in—maybe out of curiosity. Games also help to teach children how to win and lose without being prideful or pouting—a life lesson more easily received in the midst of merriment.

Vacations are valuable. These annual family adventures make memories that everyone can share. They are special times when schedules and appointments are put on hold and togetherness becomes top priority. Laughing, learning, and communicating create deeper, more meaningful connections.

For us, camping was a family favorite. It was definitely a great way to create bonding moments. There is nothing quite like a family huddling together in a soaked tent to help them bond. We experienced this on numerous occasions! Camping is also a great way to accomplish tasks together such as cooking, setting up a tent, and hiking through the woods. If you have never gone camping, give it a try. And get ready for some enjoyable, "in-tents" moments!

Having fun as a family infuses life-giving energy into your relationships, and children really are a lot of fun!

Traditions are a treasure. Holiday customs and birthday celebrations can go a long way to unite a family. Our family enjoyed a hike in the woods every Thanksgiving morning. Everyone grabbed their hiking boots first thing and headed to the woods to see what we could see. It served as a quick break from the bustle of getting ready for the big meal.

Christmastime can also be fun. Putting up decorations, trimming the tree, wrapping gifts, and singing along to favorite songs are just a few things that make the holidays enjoyable. But you don't have to wait for the holidays to make a tradition. Our family had a tradition of fixing tacos when our favorite football team was on TV. We put on any football paraphernalia we had and rooted for the home team. Take some time to brainstorm with your kids and invent your own traditions. They will love it!

Bottom line: Have fun! What can you and your kids do to have fun? To help you get some good ideas, make it a topic of conversation during your family mealtimes. Simply go around the table and ask for each person's input. Jot down the ideas in a notebook and take turns choosing. Some families like to play miniature golf or go bowling, while others enjoy a game of basketball or a day at the beach. Remember, the goal is to have fun with the family. Therefore, it is wise not to pick a highly competitive activity that might cause someone to feel bad if they don't do well.

Interestingly, family fun times also serve as some of the most teachable moments in our children's lives. They help impart the value of being respectful of other people's choices whether those choices are liked or not. They also help remind us to lighten up and have a good time. If you think about it, life is really short. The average life span is about eighty years. Percentage wise, your time to parent your kids is quite small. So enjoy your children. They truly are a special gift on loan to you from God. Don't let the time slip away.

LEARN TO LAUGH

Good humor produces laughter, and laughter is vital to families. With our fast-paced society, we can bring a lot of stress into our homes, and laughter is a great way to release it. When we laugh, our body releases a number of endorphins and neurotransmitters that make us feel good. Consequently, this reduces our levels of stress hormones. Indeed, "A happy heart is good medicine and a cheerful mind works healing..." (Proverbs 17:22 AMP).

Studies show that families who laugh together tend to have a positive outlook on life (not to mention a source of free entertainment). One study actually found that parents who use humor were the most effective.3 Research also reveals that humor helps to reduce tension and quarrelling. It can be used to express care, put family members at ease, and help everyone cope with difficult or stressful situations.4

Even Sigmund Freud recognized the importance of laughter in his book *Jokes and Their Relation to the Unconscious.* He described laughter as the body's way of safely releasing anxiety, aggression, fear, and anger.5 Indeed, humor helps create an environment in which people desire to live. It relaxes the defenses and helps children and parents feel safe to be themselves. In this way, they can deal with difficult topics and avoid many of the negative side effects that often occur.

> *Family fun times serve as some of the most teachable moments in your children's lives. So learn to lighten up and laugh with your kids whenever you can!*

Humor in families can take on many forms. It may be quoting a line from a silly movie or making light of yourself for misunderstanding a situation. When I was a child, my mom would often do silly things. One of her traditions, which was handed down from my grandmother, was to dance with the vacuum sweeper. She would also make "fish faces" out of the blue for no particular reason. I carried a number of her antics into my parenting and created a few of my own.

When our son was little, I liked to play with him by bumping into him while walking in the hall. Of course, he would retaliate with a nudge of his own. Occasionally, my husband and I would pretend to be a rock star strumming an imaginary guitar. Sometimes the "guitar" was our three or four year old. We would hold them on our lap and strum their tummy. Singing off key while driving for no apparent reason also drew many laughs. Half the fun in all this was watching the kids respond to our humor. Sometimes they rolled their eyes at our silliness, but often they came up with silliness of their own.

Sleepovers at our house were also a blast. Often, when it was time to get up in the morning, our children and their friends would not budge. I would knock on the door or turn on the light and announce that they needed to "rise and shine." Unfortunately, I was usually greeted with moans, groans, and pillows pulled over heads. When they did get up, their mood was not a happy one.

Then one day I heard a song on a children's television program called, "When Ducks Get Up in the Morning," and I decided to use it to wake them up. It is a humorous little jingle, and after I sang the existing verses, I made up many of my own. In fact, I made up a verse for each child that fit their "wake-up personas." If they still weren't stirring after all of this, I would add another verse about when our *dog* gets up in the morning—followed by our *cat*, *bird*, etc. Initially the kids moaned and groaned, but eventually I heard them giggling. I think I found it more amusing than they did, so at least I was entertaining myself!

After several mornings of singing that song, they pleaded with me not to sing it again. Eventually, this became an ongoing joke between our children and their friends. One day I overheard them laughing and saying, "Man, if we don't get up when we're called, my mom will sing us this totally obnoxious song." As the years went by, they still "hated" the song. But every time they heard it, they sprang out of bed saying, "We're up! Please don't sing that song!"

Recently, I was at the wedding of one of our children's friends, and he was telling his fiancé about the times he spent the night at our house. Of course, the song was reminisced and even recited. Humor definitely made a better memory of getting up than if we had irritated them with harsh warnings.

Indeed, humor is a powerful way to cultivate your relationships. I encourage you to incorporate it as often as you can. Just remember not to use humor to put-down other family members or get a laugh at someone else's expense. This can be very costly and leave lasting negative effects. So learn to laugh with your children in a healthy way and reap its rich rewards.

Humor is a powerful way to cultivate your relationships. It reduces tension, puts family members at ease, and helps everyone cope with stressful situations.

EXPRESS HIGH VALUE TO YOUR CHILD

Intentionally spending time with your children is an awesome way to cultivate your relationship. It not only says "I love you," but also "You have great value." More than just words, it shows them through your actions that you admire and believe in them.

Stop and think. Have you ever really admired someone? I certainly have. I knew a lady that I greatly respected and trusted whose wisdom seemed profound. Because of my deep respect, I longed for her to consider me in the same way. I wanted her to notice me, and I wanted to be a part of her inner circle of friends. Whatever she was doing or thinking, I was interested in, and I never missed an opportunity to accept an invitation to join her. I believe we need this same kind of admiration for our children!

GO ON SPECIAL DATES TOGETHER

One way to express high value and cultivate your relationship is to *date your child* individually. Find something the two of you can do together—something that involves that one child and yourself. An example would be to take him or her out to breakfast. Resist the temptation to bring the whole family. There are times for that too, but this is a date with just one child. If you have several children, make plans to take each one out on his or her own date fairly soon.

Each special date is a great opportunity for conversation to flow and to learn what is going on in his or her world. It gives them time to privately share their thoughts and feelings uninterrupted. The scenario that Dr. Dobson talked about at the opening of this chapter would be considered a "date" because it was an event shared by just he and his father.

ATTEND THEIR EVENTS

One of the most important things you can do as a parent is to be there for your kids. This includes attending as many of the activities they are involved in as you can. If your daughter is involved in dance or music and has a recital, go to it—even if you don't like it. Learn as much as you can about what they like, and learn to appreciate it. One of the saddest scenes I have witnessed is to see a child or teen look into the audience while at their play, game, or recital, and discover that their parents are not there.

My husband, Don, had a high-pressured job with a lot of responsibilities. Our son Alan played sports, and his games were always after school. In spite of Don's demanding schedule and his forty-five minute drive home, he always seemed to find a way to make it to our son's games. Don's father had done the same for him when he was playing ball. He remembers looking up in the stands and seeing his father at every game. He doesn't recall him ever missing, which meant the world to him.

Likewise, it meant the world to Alan that his dad sacrificed to be at his games. It showed him that he was a high priority and that his father's words meant something. My prediction is that Alan will make his children's events a priority also.

> *Two ways to express high value to your child is to go on special dates together and attend their activities.*

Friend, don't miss the opportunities to express high value to your kids. Join in their activities whenever you can when it is appropriate. What a great opportunity to display how much you care about the things they care about.

Like a friend you admire, ask for their opinion and respect what they have to say. This is a great way to bond and show them respect. There will be many times when discipline and instruction won't be required. All they'll need is your presence. So be intentional and pursue cultivating a relationship with them. As you learn how to hang out and enjoy their company, communication will flow more easily!

*There will be many times when discipline
and instruction won't be required.
All they will need is your presence.*

Endnotes

[1]Gary Chapman and Ross Campbell, *The 5 Love Languages of Children* (Chicago, IL: Northfield Publishing, 2012) p. 17.

[2]Rolf Zettersten, *Turning Hearts Toward Home* (Word Publishing, 1989) p. 26.

[3]Adapted from the study "The Relationship Between Humor and Family Strengths," by Jon Leonard Wuerffel, 1986.

[4]Ibid.

[5]"Laughter: Let It Out, Be Healthy," by Valerie Brett (http://www.econosystems.com/Articles/laughter.htm, accessed 10/2/13).

Reflection and Application

1. Every child—regardless of gender, nationality, or age—spells love TIME. Are you intentionally pursuing your child? If not, why? What can you adjust (or sacrifice) in your life to make time to spend with them?

   _____

   _____

   _____

   Are you frustrated or aggravated with your child? Go to God and surrender your hurts to Him. Ask Him to forgive you for holding onto any unforgiveness, and ask Him to pour fresh love into your heart to love them unconditionally.

2. Humor generates laughter and helps bring healing and happiness to your home. Do you and your children laugh together? If so, how often? What kinds of silly things make your kids laugh? What practical things can you do to experience more lightheartedness in your home?

   _____

   _____

   _____

   For questions 1 and 2, take a few moments to pray. Get God involved by asking Him for wisdom to see the things you need to see and remember what you need to remember.

3. Have you ever taken your children out *individually* for a special date? It doesn't have to be expensive to be fun. Stop and think. What are some practical outings you can go on with each of your kids to connect with them and cultivate your relationship?

   _____

   _____

   _____

   Ideas may include going to the park, getting an ice cream cone, or visiting local attractions in your city that offer free admission. Be creative. Be adventurous. Explore your options!

"… The atmosphere of the home, including verbal and non-verbal communication from parents, plays a significant role in shaping a child's identity and behavior. ….The more you understand your child's uniqueness, the better prepared you will be to nurture him with your words."

—H. Norman Wright[1]

Chapter 5

The Power of Communication

"Words kill, words give life; they're either
poison or fruit—you choose."
Proverbs 18:21 The Message

In the last chapter, we talked about the need for cultivation. Taking the time to listen, talk with, and interact with your child is the first building block to a good relationship. The second one works hand in hand with the first and it is *Communication*.

Without question, your words are powerful. They are either giving life to your children or producing death. Therefore, it is vital that you learn how to harness for good the fruit of your lips. It is also important to understand how your child communicates in order to connect with them effectively.

Like adults, children can be very different when it comes to communication. Navigating these differences can sometimes be quite challenging. Usually, kids seem to fall into one of two categories. They either tell all there is to know and more, or they give the minimal information required. I call the first group the "Spare No Details" kids, and the second group is the "Just the Facts" kids.

If you have two or more children, you probably have at least one in each group, and you know what I am talking about.

> *Your words are powerful. They are either giving life to your children or producing death.*

"Spare No Details"
Kids

The Spare No Details kids thrive on information. When you ask them how their day was, they will tell you—often giving you more information than you want to know. Typically, girls are more detailed in their conversation than boys. But some boys can be just as detailed. Kids in this group will often share what happened between them and their friends. "He said this, and she said that. Then I did this, and they did that. She was wearing this, and I was wearing that. And we ate…" and on and on they go.

Spare No Details kids tend to wear their heart on their sleeve. They tell you what they feel and what they think. They are like those boats with an outboard motor we discussed in chapter 1. What makes them tick and what drives them is clear and easy to see.

Unfortunately, I have watched children and teens in this group grow silent because they feel their parents are not listening to what they have to say. The unspoken message they hear is: "My life is not important to them. What interests me has little meaning to them." Even though their parents don't mean to send this message, it is the message their kids are hearing.

If you have a Spare No Details child, it is very important to listen to what they are saying, even though it may seem trivial. Make eye contact while they are speaking and give them your attention. This lets them know you are interested in what they have to say and you respect them for telling you.

Spare No Details kids thrive on information and tend to wear their heart on their sleeve.

"JUST THE FACTS" Kids

On the opposite end of the spectrum, we find the Just the Facts kids. These children specialize in one-word answers. A conversation with them might sound something like this:

Parent: "How was your day?"

Child: "Fine."

Parent: "What did you do?"

Child: "Nothing."

Many parents with Just the Facts kids compare communicating with them with pulling teeth. Extracting their child's true thoughts and feelings is often a painful process. After a while, they grow tired of asking multiple questions and getting the same one-word response.

Unfortunately, Just the Facts kids tend to listen the same way they communicate. Just as they are short on *giving* details, they are also short on *hearing* details. Their attention is easily distracted, allowing their mind to quickly wander off. They are not interested in what is being communicated, so they don't engage.

There are various reasons that children fall into this group. The most obvious is that they are wired this way. A Morse code style of communication is embedded in their personality. Genetically, they are more introverted and tend to internalize their thoughts and emotions. If this describes your child, you need to respect how God made them. But, at the same time, you can learn how to draw them out so you can connect and develop a relationship with them.

Another reason children fall into the Just the Facts category is *personal choice*. A number of them have opened up in the past and were hurt in the process. To protect themselves from being hurt again, they choose to share only what is necessary. Some are hurting so deeply inside that they don't know how to express themselves at all. They hold their thoughts and feelings close to their heart, and unless their parents carefully draw the pain out, the child may never experience the healing and closure they desperately need.

Thankfully, there are practical ways to connect with your kids when they are reluctant to communicate.

Just the Facts kids specialize in one-word answers.
For various reasons, they hold their thoughts and
feelings close to their heart and are
reluctant to communicate.

THREE GUIDELINES
FOR COMMUNICATING WITH YOUR CHILD

1. Use Open-ended Questions.

Open-ended questions are those that cannot be answered with one-word, yes or no answers. They require detailed information. For instance, instead of asking, "How was your day?" You can say, "Tell me about your day. Who did you hang around at lunch? What was the favorite thing you did?" Another good question to encourage communication is, "What was that like for you when…" or "How did that make you feel?" The key here is to engage them and encourage them to open up.

2. Clarify Your Child's Statements.

Clarifying a statement means to repeat what your child said, but not necessarily in the exact same words. For instance, let's say your son or daughter tells you about a struggle they had with two of their friends. You could clarify what the struggle was and say, "I bet you felt like you were between a rock and a hard place." Statements like these are non-judgmental and encourage your child to express themselves while conveying your interest.

3. Be an Effective Listener.

A third way to communicate and connect with your child is by becoming an effective listener. While effective listening includes the use of open-ended questions and clarifying statements, it is largely about non-verbal communication. Ironically, your non-verbal communication makes up about 80 percent of your response to the person with whom you are speaking.

Have you ever spoken with someone who was watching TV? You tried to share something important you wanted them to know, and they never looked up once. Their eyes stayed glued to the tube. Eventually, you began to wonder if they had heard anything you said. What message did that send to you? Did you feel valued? I doubt it.

Effective listening shows that you care about the person speaking. It involves making and maintaining *good eye contact* throughout your conversation. In this case, eye contact with your child lets them know you are listening and that they are important. *Positive facial expressions* and *body posture* are also essential.

---

*Three guidelines for communicating with your child
include using open-ended questions, clarifying their
statements, and being an effective listener.*

Facial expressions help them determine how you feel about what they are saying. Your expressions show that you are concerned, sad, angry, etc., as it relates to the discussion. Rolling your eyes or looking the other way will be tell-tale signs of possible disgust or disbelief.

Body posture also reflects how valuable they are. If you are leaning forward in your chair and making eye contact, you are showing that you are listening intently. If your side or back is toward them, you are showing that your focus is on something else and not on them. And your children pick up on this at an amazingly young age.

Our two-year old grandson has already grasped the meaning of good, non-verbal communication. When he has caught us glancing at the paper or texting a friend while he is talking, he will press his little hands on our face and say, "Look at me with your eyes!" It is amazing to me how they grasp our non-verbal skills!

A good rule of thumb in communication is the golden rule given by Jesus: "In everything, do to others what you would have them do to you…" (Matthew 7:12). If you would like your children's undivided attention, give it to them. If you want them to look at you while you are speaking, look at them while they are speaking. What you give to them in the form of good eye contact, facial expressions, and body posture are *seeds* you are sowing from which you will one day reap a harvest. If you want to reap good communication, you've got to plant it.

> *Giving your kids good eye contact, facial expressions, and body posture are seeds you are sowing from which one day you will reap a harvest.*

SHOW RESPECT IN YOUR COMMUNICATION

What's true of good communication is also true of respect. If you *want* respect, you have to *give* respect. Effective listening and clarifying are ways to show your children respect. Asking for their opinion is another way. For instance, let's say you are rearranging the living room. You could ask, "What do you think would be the best way to arrange the furniture?" Or maybe they share with you about a friend who ran into trouble at school. You could ask, "What do you think John should have done when the teacher accused him of cheating?" These kinds of questions not only show that you value their opinion, but also get them to think!

This reminds me of a situation that happened with our daughter, Stephanie, when she was three. We had been visiting my parents who lived about five hours away and were leaving the next day to head back home. My mom asked if Stephanie could spend a few days with them. Normally, we would just make the decision for her, but this time we decided to let her make it.

My mom asked Stephanie to take a walk with her so that she could invite her to stay a few extra days. They then discussed the pros and cons of the decision together.

"Mommy and daddy won't be here to tuck you in at night," G'ma said, "or hold you if you get home sick. On the other hand, you will get to spend some special time with G'ma and G'pa. We will feed the birds together, and G'pa will probably make your favorite pancakes—the ones with the syrup face on them."

This was a big decision for Stephanie—a tough choice indeed. When given the opportunity to make the choice, it was fun to see her little wheels turning as she examined both sides of her options. At last, she breathed a sigh and said, "G'ma, I think that I'm a big enough girl to stay with you for a couple of days."

When given the chance, you must allow your children to think and make decisions on their own. These choices need to be safe and age-appropriate. Allowing them to make some decisions does not mean they are in control of the family or rule the household. It means you are giving them respect to make decisions and helping them learn how to make them properly.

For example, if you have a young child, you can allow them to choose which outfit they want to wear for the day. "Would you like to wear the red shirt and blue shorts or the green shirt with your jeans?" Likewise, you can give your child the choice of which chore he would like to do first. "Would you like to feed the dog first or take out the trash?"

Again, allowing your children to think and make decisions on their own shows respect, and you must give respect if you want to receive it. Remember, children are little people who have the same basic needs as adults. They want to feel valued, respected, and be heard. Granting them respect and expecting respect will help them mature into respectful adults.

Allowing your children to think and make decisions on their own shows respect, and you must give respect if you want to receive it.

COMMUNICATE YOUR FAITH

Your faith is one of the most important things you can communicate to your child. Of all the life lessons you share, none are more powerful than your personal testimony. How has the Lord helped you in your struggles? What has He been teaching you lately? Sharing these things with your child in a way they can understand is a great way to share your beliefs and make them real.

When I was a child, I remember a time when my dad lost his job. To make ends meet, he had to take a job that he actually hated. I watched him struggle like I had never seen him struggle before. During that season, my mom and dad would pray and ask the Lord for direction. Dad didn't always handle the situation in a godly way. Yet, while I saw his faults and frailties, I also witnessed the power of prayer and forgiveness.

In the midst of great pain, my parents continued to seek guidance from the Lord. Through their testimony, I learned that life can sometimes be hard, but the Lord will always be there for us in our struggles. This lesson was more profound than any lesson from a book. It was God interacting in a real-life situation—our situation.

I have seen families take their children to church and expect the church to teach them about the Lord, yet never mention Him at home. But what is that teaching them? What are kids supposed to do with what they learn at church if they don't apply it in their lives? In order to truly connect them in a relationship with God, we have to allow God to be a part of all that we do every day—not just a sixty-minute segment on Sunday morning.

I encourage you to communicate your faith with your kids by sharing real-life stories of how God has helped you in the past. If you are presently struggling with something, share with them an appropriate overview of what's going on. Ask them for their opinion if it is applicable, and ask them to pray for you.

Sharing the challenges and imperfections that you are working through makes you a real person in your children's eyes. It helps to remove the stigma that parents are (or think they are) perfect and have all the answers. It not only shows your kids respect, but also lets them know it is okay to struggle at times. As you seek to be real and transparent and communicate your faith, you will help connect your kids with God in a way that nothing else can.

> *Communicate your faith with your*
> *kids by sharing real-life stories.*
> *Nothing is more powerful.*

SCHOOL DAZE
A Real-Life Story Illustrating the Power of Your Words

I was very fortunate to grow up in a home where I knew I was loved and valued. My parents instilled in me that I could be anything I wanted to be. Again and again, they told me that they were excited to see how the Lord would use me to bless others. Through their words, they communicated to me that I had gifts and talents, and I just needed to work hard to achieve my goals. Of course, I believed them. They were my parents…they were adults. I was taught to respect them as well as all adults who had authority over me.

Time passed and I entered grade school. But it wasn't as easy as I assumed it would be. My parents had told me repeatedly that I was smart, so I couldn't figure out why I had to work so hard. My neighbor, who was in my class, always seemed to breeze through her homework. While I was struggling to finish, she would often show up at my house and begin throwing pebbles at my window. "Aren't you done yet, Peggy?" she'd say. "Come on out and play."

In my mind, the logical answer to my learning dilemma was quite simple. "All the other kids, including my friend, are using up all their brain power now," I explained to my mom and dad. "They won't have any left when they grow up. But I will! I'm saving it for when I am an adult!" Regardless of my conclusions, my teachers made some conclusions of their own.

THE GREAT SEPARATION

Back in my day, it was not out of the ordinary for a teacher to break up her class into three groups. There was the smart group, the average group, and the dumb group. I know there were silent prayers being prayed throughout the classroom as the teacher started dividing the class. Although the groups were not verbally or physically labeled *smart*, *average*, and *dumb*, everyone knew what the groups were and which one they fell in. Nobody wanted to be placed in the dumb group.

A similar situation took place in gym class, only in this case it was the students who decided the groups. On the days when we played team sports, the gym teacher would pick two captains, and they would take turns picking the kids they wanted on their team. "Pick me! Pick me!" came the loud, desperate screams as the team captains scanned the line looking for the biggest and most talented kid who could help him win.

Again, silent prayers were offered—this time by the scrawny kids of which I was one. I loved to play sports, and I especially loved kickball and dodge ball. But as much as I loved it, I was too scrawny to make a good kick or throw. Oh, how I hated team selection time. Having to sit and watch all the other kids get picked before me was humiliating.

No matter how much we wanted to be picked, us scrawny kids wouldn't dare try to convince the captains to pass on all of the great players and go with us. Instead, we begged silently in our hearts, *Please, please, please pick me! Please don't let me be the last one to be picked. Please!* Being picked last was the worst fate of all for a grade schooler! Something I experienced more times than I can count.

I still remember the deep disappointment on the captains' faces when they realized they were stuck with the worst player there. A concert of jeers and sneers went up as the rest of the team joined forces and voiced their disapproval. The message was loud and clear: "Nobody wants you. Nobody thinks you're good enough. Everyone knows when the most crucial play of the game comes it will be *your* turn, and you will be the one who makes the out that causes the team to lose. Why did we have to get stuck with you?"

THE FOOLISH TEACHER

For me, fourth grade was the worst of all. My teacher's name was Miss Wendy. She was young and beautiful, and I really looked forward to having her as my teacher. That year was election year, and my aunt decided to make me a special dress for school. To honor our Republican heritage, she put an elephant's face on the front of it and an elephant's rear on the back—complete with a small tassel for a tail. I was so proud of the dress and proud of my aunt for making it for me.

Little did I know what that dress would do. I still remember seeing the disgust on Miss Wendy's face as she stared at that elephant coming into her classroom for the first time. Evidently, she was a dyed-in-the-wool Democrat who hated Republicans. It seemed as if she felt it was her God-given right to take out her disgust on an innocent little fourth grader.

From then on, my teacher no longer called me by my first name like all the other children. I was now called by my last name—if I was called on at all. And when she did call on me, it was not in the sweet tone she used with the rest of the class. Instead, she voiced my name as if I were something vile and evil. When we divided up into our groups, I was abruptly transferred to the dumb group on a consistent basis.

Fear began to grip me. All of a sudden, I hated school. A number of kids picked up on Miss Wendy's treatment and assumed that there was something wrong with me. I now had no first name and was placed in the dumb group. As a result, some of them began jeering at me by imitating the teacher. They would make a face at me while hollering my last name, "Holloway! Holloway!" Miss Wendy did nothing. Instead of telling them to quit, she acted as though I deserved to be made the brunt of their jokes.

Upon hearing what was happening, my mom talked to the principal. He told her he would speak to Miss Wendy but concluded that I must have been exaggerating. My mom encouraged me to overlook her behavior and trust my teacher and principal. "Everything's going to be okay," she said. But it wasn't.

Shortly thereafter, the principal spoke to Miss Wendy to let her know of the complaint. This only made things worse. Instead of backing off, she increased her efforts, calling on me more often. If I answered wrong, she criticized me, and if I answered right, I was ignored.

Humiliated, I went to my parents again and explained what was happening. Thank God they believed me. As horrible as the situation was, how much worse would it have been had they not believed me or ignored my cries. I am so grateful I had a relationship with them and they took the time to know my heart and see that it was broken. I was not exaggerating; I was telling the truth.

Back to school they went, this time requesting that I be transferred to another class. But the request was denied. They then asked for a parent-teacher conference with me present, and it was granted. During the meeting, I watched and listened as Miss Wendy talked to my mom and dad. "Peggy's just an average girl," she said. "Average is all that she is and ever will be."

Her words cut like a knife straight to my heart. All the love and value I had received from my parents had been tainted by the words of my fourth grade teacher. My mind began to wonder, *My parents aren't teachers. Miss Wendy is probably right. After all, she is a teacher and probably knows these things from her professional experience. My mom and dad have to say nice things because they are my parents and they love me. What else can they say? Therefore, I must be average, and average is all I will be for the rest of my life. And besides, who is going to want a scrawny kid on their team anyway—especially if they're just going to be average at what they do...even in the things they love to do.*

That is the message I received from fourth grade. It seems I didn't have the inner strength like some people do. I couldn't just blow off my teacher's words. I carried them with me through most of my adult life. Thank God the sting has finally been removed.

As a parent, caregiver, or teacher, please be very careful what you say to the children under your care. You have the power of life and death in your tongue. You can help mold them in a positive way or a negative way. I encourage you to choose your words wisely. Be constructive, not destructive. Let the words of your lips bring life, and your children will be blessed!

Endnotes

[1]H. Norman Wright, *The Power of a Parent's Words* (Ventura, CA: Regal Books, a division of GL Publications, 1991) pp. 28-29; 13.

Reflection and Application

1. As a parent, your words are powerful in your child's life. Stop and think. What kinds of words or phrases come out of your mouth most frequently (when you are calm and when you are upset)? Are they life-giving? What do you feel prompted to change?

   _____

   _____

   Get God involved. Ask Him for wisdom to see the things you need to see and remember what you need to remember.

2. Carefully read Philippians 4:8. Now stop and think, *What qualities of my child are true, honorable, right, pure, lovely, good, excellent, and worthy of praise?* Take time to list as many as you can think of, and then ask the Lord to help you fix your mind on them.

   _____

   _____

   Pause and pray: "Lord, please allow the good in my child to outshine their areas of immaturity. May these qualities influence my thinking and feelings and find their way into my words. Help me to speak life and not death to them. In Jesus' name, Amen."

3. Think back over your life. Did you have a similar experience with a teacher like Miss Wendy? If so, briefly describe what happened and how it made you feel.

   _____

   _____

   If the hurtful words of a past teacher or your parents still ring in your ears, allow God's Spirit to bring healing to your heart. Simply pray and tell Him how you feel and ask Him to take away the pain. He loves you more than words can say! Check out these encouraging passages in Scripture: Psalm 34:17-19; 139:13-18; Jeremiah 29:11.

"...If you are willing to learn, your children will teach you more about parenting than you will ever discover in books. You can't beat on-the-job training! ...Long ago, I learned there are no perfect parents or perfect children. It is reassuring to discover the average child can absorb all of the mistakes of the average parent without any lasting damage. Isn't that a relief!"

—**Dr. Richard D. Dobbins**[1]

The Importance of Observation

"Young people eventually reveal by their actions
if their motives are on the up and up."
Proverbs 20:11 *The Message*

*T*hus far, we have explored the first two building blocks of a good relationship—cultivation and communication. The third block is also vitally important and is seamlessly connected with the first two. It is *observation*.

In order to truly know *who* you are developing a relationship with, you must take the time to observe them. What you see on the surface is not always an accurate reflection of what is inside a person's heart. This holds true for your child as well.

MEET "DEBBIE"

Debbie was a talented young girl at our church when I was growing up. Her father was a deacon, and her mother was actively involved in missions. Debbie's ability to play the piano for Sunday services gained her great respect in the eyes of all parents. Sons were encouraged to date her, and daughter's parents were set at ease when they heard Debbie was going to be at the function their child was begging to attend.

Debbie's reputation provided a great smokescreen for us to go places we shouldn't go and do things we shouldn't do. What parents did not realize was that Debbie's ability to play the piano and her parent's church involvement did not exclude her from being a youth like the rest of us. They only looked at the outside package. Although things looked good, Debbie was just as human as the rest of us and just as capable of getting into trouble!

How can you truly know your child? Do you go by what you see on the outside? Can you accurately measure their character by the grades they make? What about their words? Are these a true reflection of who they are? While all these indicators are helpful, we must dig a bit deeper to reveal the real deal.

To truly know who your child is, you must take the time to observe them. What you see on the surface is not always an accurate reflection of what is inside their heart.

BECOME A DETECTIVE

In order to get a good glimpse into the heart of your child, you must become a detective. For starters, you must observe what attracts their attention. The things that attract and hold their interest say a lot about their heart's desires. If you sense it is something unhealthy, you can help redirect their focus.

If you have concerns that your child is engaging in more harmful behavior, it would be very wise to search their room when they are not around. But be careful to leave things as you found them. If they suspect you have been in their room, they will find a better way to hide what you are looking for the next time. I know this might sound bizarre, but in some cases, a parent being nosey could save their child's life.

Throughout my many years of counseling, I have discovered five "vital signs" for you to observe to get a clearer understanding of your child's mental, emotional, and spiritual health. These are five things in your child's life that you should know that are shaping their character and directing them into adulthood.

1. Know Your Child's *Friends*.

A youth pastor once told me, "If you want to know who your kids are, see who their friends are." That is very good advice— advice that reflects the importance of the sayings, "Water seeks its own level" and "Birds of a feather flock together." If your child is hanging out with kids who are doing drugs, chances are your child is doing drugs too. Likewise, if your child is hanging out with kids involved in shoplifting, you more than likely have a shoplifter living with you.

The Bible is pretty clear about the power of friends. First Corinthians 15:33 says, "Don't fool yourselves. Bad friends will destroy you" (CEV). And Proverbs 13:20 declares, "Become wise by walking with the wise; hang out with fools and watch your life fall to pieces" (The Message).

I hear some parents complain when their children want to have friends over. My husband, Don, and I were thrilled when our children wanted to ask friends to come to our house. That provided an opportunity to see who their friends were and what they enjoyed doing. By simply observing their interaction, we could see who was leading the group and where our child fit in.

> *"Become wise by walking with the wise; hang out with fools and watch your life fall to pieces."*
> —*Proverbs 13:20 The Message*

When I was growing up, my parents were kind to my friends and always glad to see them. They would invite them into our home and ask how they were doing. Out of genuine care and concern, my mom and dad would use every opportunity to point them to the Lord and help them see their true value—just as the Lord sees them. Even after I left for college, my friends still came to visit my parents on occasion because they knew they were loved by them.

During my years of parenting, I thoroughly enjoyed the kids that passed through our doors. Like my parents, I tried to set the same standard—an atmosphere of unconditional love and care that said, "Welcome! I'm glad to see you."

I strongly encourage you to make your home an accessible, fun environment for your children and their friends. One mother who took this advice told me she would make cookies when her kids' friends came over. The cookies were never turned away, and guess who delivered them? That's right—Mom. And she was usually invited to enter their domain and could observe what was happening.

Some of the kids may ask you to join in an activity or conversation. That happened to us a number of times. It is fine to join in on occasion, but I would advise you to be sensitive to how your child feels about your participation. This is another way to show them respect. Remember, these young people are your kids' friends, not yours. If they feel uncomfortable with your participation, they will refrain from inviting their friends to the house.

So take time to know your kids' friends and be a part of their lives. Welcome them into your home when you can, and then *observe* their behavior. Do they welcome your presence or fear it? What kind of things do they talk about? What kind of things do they do? Are they respectful of authority, and most importantly what kind of relationship do they have with God? Answering questions like these will give you a good gauge on your child's heart as well as the direction in which they are headed. If counsel is needed to direct them to better friends, it will be evident.

> *Know your kids' friends. Make your home an accessible, fun environment for them and your children.*

2. KNOW YOUR CHILD'S *CHOICE OF MUSIC.*

Music is a powerful motivator, and the type of music your child listens to is a big indicator of who they are. The same is true of television, film, and other media choices. These reflect their personality and value system. If your child is drawn to music that talks about murdering parents and cops or sexual abuse, you should delve deeper and inquire as to why. Something is going on in their heart that needs to be brought to the surface and dealt with properly and prayerfully.

One exciting trend I have noticed is an increased popularity in contemporary Christian music. It is well-liked by Christian kids and teens as well as adults. The message is positive and the music is upbeat. Families are cranking it up in their cars and attending concerts together. In fact, it is helping many parents and teens cross barriers that have separated them for decades. The lyrics keep God in the center of their lives, helping to produce grateful hearts. It gives hope to the hopeless and heals the brokenhearted. Contemporary Christian music is even "cool" and acceptable to many peers who have not heard it before.

If you find that your children could benefit from listening to some new and improved tunes, I suggest checking out contemporary Christian music. There is likely one or more CCM stations in your area, and the Internet has a wealth of good music to offer. Online streaming and phone apps have made finding good music much easier.

3. KNOW YOUR CHILD'S *CHOICE OF CLOTHES.*

Clothes are a huge statement as to who your child is and who they want to be. This is especially true of most girls who openly express who they are by what they wear. Indeed, clothes are not only a fashion statement, they are also an indicator of what is going on in your child's heart—especially regarding purity.

For example, if your daughter tells you she desires abstinence and a pure dating relationship, yet dresses provocatively, she may be giving you a clue as to what is really in her heart. On the other hand, if you notice she is careful to buy jeans that are not too tight and shirts that are not too low cut, she is likely sending a message that purity is important to her.

Although boys are not as big on clothes as girls, you can still get an idea of what's going on in their heart and what type of crowd they are attempting to attract by what they want to wear. If they desire clothes with multiple rips, stains, and holes, it would be good to find out why. Likewise, if your son or daughter is attracted to an all-black, Goth look or apparel that is plastered with skulls and crossbones, there is a reason for it, and you need to learn what it is.

To a great degree, what we wear on the outside is a reflection of how we think and feel on the inside. So get to know your child's choice of clothes. This will give you a glimpse inside their heart like few things will.

Know your child's choice of music and clothes.
They give you a good glimpse
inside their heart.

---

4. KNOW YOUR CHILD'S *PERSONALITY*.

One of your child's vital signs that bears watching is the development of their *personality*. By definition, personality is "the combination of characteristics or qualities that form an individual's distinctive character."[2] Your child's character is uncovered through observation. The Bible says, "The *character* of even a child can be known by the way he acts—whether what he does is pure and right" (Proverbs 20:11 TLB). Watching and listening to how they conduct themselves among their peers and siblings as well as with people in authority like you, will tell you a lot about what is in their heart and who they are becoming.

Keep in mind that the formation of your child's personality will be greatly influenced by the friends they hang around and the media that entertains them. Helping them connect with good, godly friends, make healthy media choices, and discover the truth of God's Word, will go a long way to positively shape their personality. Their teachers and your role as their parent are also factors in the mix.

So keep an eye on their personality. Observe what their disposition and temperament is. How do they interact with others?

What do they do in their spare time? Are they a leader or a follower? What is motivating them to do good or bad? Answers to questions like these will help you keep a pulse on their true heartbeat and make careful and prayerful course adjustments to their life.

5. KNOW YOUR CHILD'S *CHOICE OF COMPUTER SITES.*

The computer can be a wonderful tool for education, but it can also be very damaging if not monitored. Pornography and gambling are both highly addictive and easily accessible—especially in the privacy of a child's room when no parent or guardian is watching. Online chat rooms have also become problematic places for a number of kids.

If you are concerned that your child is visiting unhealthy sites, you should check the computer's history of sites visited. I would also encourage you to take a look at their social media page and/ or email account if they have one. This is another very good indicator of their character. Many parents have been shocked when they've accessed their child or teen's media pages and read the posts.

The bottom line is, you need to monitor their computer time. One suggestion I have heard that is worth considering is placing the computer with Internet access in a family room, not in a bedroom or secluded area. This keeps the screen in full view and helps everyone be more accountable for the sites they are surfing. Another suggestion is to limit Internet access on your child or teen's phone to only when they are with you (or eliminate it altogether). These are choices you will need to make. Just keep in mind that "garbage in equals garbage out." So help your child guard what they put in their mind and heart, and their life will remain pointed in the right direction!

Garbage in equals garbage out. So help your child guard what they put in their mind and heart.

THUNDERSTORM IN SOUTH DAKOTA
Looking at Observation from a Different Perspective

Alan was always afraid of thunderstorms. When the thunder rolled, Alan would grab his "banky" and head to us for comfort. Many a night we would hear the pitter-patter of little feet running into our bedroom to huddle between us under the covers. We tried comforting him with the knowledge that God was with him. When that didn't work, we went to the scientific approach and explained to him what causes thunderstorms. And when that didn't work, we told him that the angels were bowling, and that was where the thunder was coming from. Unfortunately, no explanation we offered seemed to help Alan at all.

Time passed, and when Alan was seven, we took our horses to South Dakota with some friends for a camping trip. Each day we rode to different mountains and buttes, returning back to our camp at day's end. I remember on one particular morning, the sun was shining brightly, and everything pointed toward having a beautiful, promising day. Our friend Mike, who had come on the trip to do some hiking, decided he would do so behind the horses. With everyone ready and in place, we left camp.

We crossed a small creek just outside of our encampment, and Mike tip-toed across a log that was conveniently placed for hikers. We then rode into Custer State Park where "the deer and the antelope play." While there, we ate our lunch on top of a butte and watched a herd of buffalo roam.

Suddenly, the wind shifted and clouds began to replace the beautiful sunlit sky. Knowing that lightning tends to strike the highest elevation, we quickly gathered our belongings to descend the butte. Within an instant, a storm formed and seemed to be moving faster than we were. Without warning, lightning struck the spot where we had been just moments before. Then came the rain accompanied by small, hard pieces of hail which pummeled us and our horses.

At this, Alan began to whimper and wanted off his pony, which was none other than Lady. Interestingly, Lady was as enthused with the rain, wind, and hail as he was. In protest, she began prancing around. With growing despair, Alan began to cry, "I just want off my pony, mom, and I want to get out of this storm."

No explanation of angels bowling or the scientific cause for storms was going to comfort him. I had to try something different. So I pulled Lady close to my horse to comfort them both. Unfortunately, by this time my horse had begun doing her own dance to avoid being hit by the hail. There was no choice left for Alan but to be brave, take control of his pony, and get off the butte.

Once we descended and made it back to the lower level, we realized our options were limited. We could either stay out in the open field and risk getting hit by lightning, or we could head for the timbers a mile away and risk being hit by a tree that was hit by lightning. Another danger weighing heavy on our minds was the fact that horses wearing metal shoes can attract lightning. After weighing all our choices, we decided to head for the timbers.

Thankfully, we made it there safely and enjoyed the protection of the trees from the hail. But the storm continued to rage. After riding several more hours, we came to our last long hill and creek crossing. Our warm, dry camper was just on the other side. At this point, Mike was busily trying to stay up with the horses. We wanted to double up and put him on one of the horses with us, but the terrain was just too unsafe.

The horses struggled to find their footing as we climbed up the last hill. Finally, we made it to the top, and then we saw it. Our trail to the campsite was one giant, mudslide. Mike stood there speechless, drenched with mud and water. There was no other way back but through it. One by one, the horses lowered their haunches to a sitting position and slid down the long hill. Mike also lowered himself to a sitting position and carefully slid from one tree to the next. He looked like a mud-covered snowball, gathering speed and mud as he slid to the bottom of the hill.

By now, Alan was fully focused on what he needed to do to get back to the camper and doing a great job with Lady. He realized that she was just as concerned as he was, and she needed some reassurance too. Carefully, he balanced himself as she slowly picked her way down the hill.

The last obstacle to overcome was the creek, which now looked more like a raging river. There was no log to be seen to get across, and the water was high on Lady's legs, all the way up to her chest. To help her and Alan cross safely, we attached a lead rope to her halter. Alan grabbed the saddle horn and rode as we led them across. When we finally got back and into the camper, we were so thankful to be safe and have a warm bed to crawl into. Unfortunately, our desires were quickly dashed when we found that an open vent had left the bed soaked. Nevertheless, we were grateful to be back at camp.

Alan was never afraid of storms again. He learned that when a challenging situation arises that you have no control over, you need to press through it and not give into your emotions. He had to focus on controlling Lady and working through a bad situation. There was no room for attitudes or giving up. I think that is why he is not afraid. He conquered his own storm.

Like Alan, your child will one day face a challenging situation that will seem insurmountable. As a parent, you can *observe* the situation as a huge trauma, which will produce anxiety, or you can observe it as an opportunity for a valuable life lesson. I encourage you to help your child praise the Lord through their storm and learn a lesson from it.

Endnotes

[1]Dr. Richard D. Dobbins, *Venturing Into a Child's World* (Old Tappan, NJ: Fleming H. Revell Company, 1985) p. 16.
[2]Definition of *Personality* (www.oxforddictionaries.com/us/definition/american_english/personality, accessed 10/3/13).

Reflection and Application

1. Can you name your child's three closest friends? If so, who are they? How would you describe their character? How about their relationship with God? Are they respectful of their parents and those in authority?

    _____

    _____

    If you don't know who your child's closest friends, ask them who they are. If possible, invite them over individually or as a group to observe their character and how they interact with your child and each other.

2. Do you know your child's choice of music (either their favorite artist or songs)? How about their favorite Internet sites? If so, take a moment to write down their top three choices in each category. (This is also an exercise you can do with their other media choices, including TV shows, movies, etc.)

My Child's Favorite Music Choices (Artists/Albums/Songs)	My Child's Favorite Websites (Frequently Visited Places)
_____	_____
_____	_____
_____	_____
_____	_____

    If you don't know who your child's favorite music or website choices, ask them. Take some time to sit with them and allow them to explore the Internet and watch where they go. You can do the same with listening to music. If they are unfamiliar with contemporary Christian music, introduce them to it. The fact that you are taking time to sit with them and venture into their world says "I love you" and will connect you with them more closely.

3. Has your child been through a challenging situation in which there seemed to be no way out? Are they in a situation like that now? If so, briefly describe it. How might you help them observe the situation from a new, healthier perspective—one that promotes a valuable life lesson?

    _____

    _____

    _____

Part III:

The Value of Rules Can Last for a Lifetime

"Let no Christian parents fall into the delusion that Sunday School is intended to ease them of their personal duties. The first and most natural condition of things is for Christian parents to train up their own children in the nurture and admonition of the Lord."

—**Charles Haddon Spurgeon**[1]

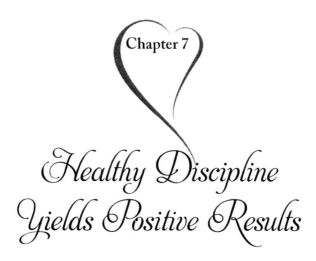

Chapter 7

Healthy Discipline Yields Positive Results

"Train a child in the way he should go, and even when he is old he will not turn away from it."
Proverbs 22:6 GW

Our relationship with our children is the foundation for our parenting. It is the first "R" in our childrearing equation. And as we have learned, the three main building blocks that make up this foundation are cultivation, communication, and observation. Through unconditional love, respect, and building good memories that are intertwined with humor, we nurture and protect our relationship.

This paves the way for the second "R" in our parenting equation which is *Rules*. Relationship plus Rules equals a passport to Instruction. These two combined enable you to "train up your child in the way they should go" and fulfill their God-given purpose.

The Encarta Dictionary defines the word *rules* as "an authoritative regulation for action, conduct, regulation, etc." Rules are necessary for structure and authority in the home, helping your children feel safe and secure in their environment. A life without rules is a disaster waiting to happen.

Essentially, Rules are discipline, and for the sake of our discussion, the two words will be used interchangeably. In this chapter, we will examine the right motive for our discipline, the difference between good and bad discipline, as well as the importance of not taking discipline lightly.

> *Rules are necessary for structure and authority in the home, helping your children feel safe and secure in their environment.*

THE MOTIVATION FOR DISCIPLINE

Motivation is the "why" behind the "what." In this case, it is "why" you are disciplining your children. What is the purpose? What are you after? In order to best answer this question, let's look at what the Bible says about God's purpose for disciplining us. Hebrews 12:6 says,

"...The Lord disciplines those he loves, and he punishes everyone he accepts as a son."

God's motivation for disciplining us is *love*. It is not anger, cruelty, or selfishness. He disciplines us because He loves us and wants us to experience the very best life we can. It is through His loving relationship with us and His discipline that we mature into His likeness. God confirms this in Hebrews 12:10 stating,

"Our fathers disciplined us for a little while as they thought best; but God disciplines us for our good, that we may share in his holiness."

As said earlier, you should never discipline your children out of anger as this does not produce the right behavior they need and you desire (see James 1:20). Like your heavenly Father, you are to discipline your children out of love with the purpose of seeing them become like God (holy). In this condition, they are positioned to experience the best life they can.

Discipline your children out of love with the purpose of seeing them become like God—holy.

THE MARKS OF DISCIPLINE

Now, all discipline is not created equal. There is good discipline and there is bad discipline. What's the difference? Let's look at Hebrews 12:11. It says,

"No discipline seems pleasant at the time, but painful. Later on, however, it produces a harvest of righteousness and peace for those who have been trained by it."

BAD DISCIPLINE IS ABUSIVE AND LEAVES SCARS.

First of all, the "pain" discussed in this verse is *not* the pain that one would inflict through anger or abuse. Please don't miss this point. I cannot emphasize it enough. Abusing a child is horrific and takes on many forms including verbal, physical, mental, emotional, and sexual abuse. Our hospitals are full of precious babies and children suffering from abuse. The visible, and more importantly *invisible*, marks it leaves on a child prove that it is *not* good discipline.

Young children are innocent and impressionable. In most cases, they don't have the ability to clearly understand what behavior is right and wrong. Yet, through abuse they suffer as though they did. Some live with emotional scars for the rest of their lives, learning lessons that are *opposite* of what the Lord desires. Abuse becomes their definition of "normal," and they will have a greater chance of abusing their own children.

Mark 9:42 warns, "If anyone causes one of these little ones who believe in me to sin, it would be better for him to be thrown into the sea with a large millstone tied around his neck." Make no mistake, abuse and discipline administered in anger is not *good* discipline and it is not what I am advocating at all.

Good Discipline Is Godly and Produces Peace and Right Living.

Again, let's carefully read Hebrews 12:11.

"No discipline seems pleasant at the time, but painful. Later on, however, it produces a harvest of righteousness and peace for those who have been trained by it."

The discipline discussed in this verse is "good" discipline. Notice that good discipline *trains*. To *train* your child means to "teach, educate, coach, instruct, guide, and prepare them." It is done in love and in control, never out of control. As you seek to "train up your child in the way he or she should go," good discipline must be part of the equation.

Now, you may look at this verse and quickly get stuck on the thought that discipline is painful, and you don't want to cause your children pain. Yes, it is painful. But note that with good discipline, the "pain" is temporary, and unlike bad discipline, it leaves *no* lasting scars. The results of good, effective discipline produce "a harvest of righteousness and peace." Who would not want that for their children?

Of course your children will probably not greet your discipline with joy. They are not going to say, "Oh, thank you so much for grounding me this weekend and taking away my heart's desires! It just means so much to me!" on the contrary, they are going to resist you. Consequently, it will be tempting to become passive and ignore their need for discipline, but don't do it. While resistance is not peaceful, the "peace" will come *after* the discipline is given—sometimes long after it.

> *Unlike bad discipline, good discipline leaves no*
> *lasting scars. Instead it produces "a harvest*
> *of righteousness and peace."*

DON'T TAKE DISCIPLINE LIGHTLY

Again, let's turn our attention to what the Bible says about discipline in Hebrews 12:5-6. It states,

"...My son, do not make light of the Lord's discipline, and do not lose heart when he rebukes you, because the Lord disciplines those he loves, and he punishes everyone he accepts as a son."

There are several points we can glean from these verses regarding discipline. First of all, it says we often "lose heart" when the Lord rebukes (corrects, disciplines) us. Yet, He does not stop, but continues to discipline. Is this because He hates us? No! He disciplines us because He loves us and "accepts us as a son."

Second, God cautions us "not to make light of" discipline. He takes His discipline of us very seriously, and He wants us to take the discipline of our children seriously too. This means your discipline needs to be planned and thought out. Wrong, unacceptable behavior and right, acceptable behavior should be clearly defined and then communicated to your children. Once they understand what is expected and you have given them a warning for disobeying, a consequence must be given.

Consequences should have a beginning and an end, and they should have one goal in mind: training them to live right(eously). With each opportunity to discipline, you should ask yourself, *How will my choice of discipline further my child's training in righteousness? How am I trying to train (teach, educate, coach, instruct, guide, and prepare) them in this particular instance?*

Wrong, unacceptable behavior and right, acceptable behavior should be clearly defined and then communicated to your children.

AN EXAMPLE FROM SCRIPTURE

Proverbs 5:7-13 is an example of a conversation a father is having with his son regarding immorality and an adulterous, loose woman. He is warning him of disaster if he does not heed his words:

"Now then, my sons, listen to me; do not turn aside from what I say. Keep to a path far from her {*the adulteress*}, do

not go near the door of her house, lest you give your best strength to others and your years to one who is cruel, lest strangers feast on your wealth and your toil enrich another man's house.

At the end of your life you will groan, when your flesh and body are spent. You will say, "How I hated discipline! How my heart spurned correction! I would not obey my teachers or listen to my instructors."

Here, a dad is telling his son, "Listen to me. What I am going to tell you is very important. Stay away from seductive women. If a married woman comes on to you, don't go anywhere near her. Don't go anywhere near her house lest you be tempted to go inside. She will give you grief and take all your money. She does not have your best interest in mind and will ruin your life. Save yourself for God's best and don't throw it away on a loose woman."

As we read this story, it appears that Junior may have rolled his eyes at dad. Maybe he put his hand up and said, "Whatever," and stomped off toward the door. The father gave him a parting warning and said, "Look son, if you don't obey me, you will regret it later. You hate discipline and you don't want anyone to tell you what to do—not your parents or your teachers. But, take heed and listen to our words and our discipline!"

In verse 14, Dad tells his son what he is going to say at the end of his life if he rejects the discipline being offered: "I have come to the brink of utter ruin…." In the closing verse of this same chapter, the Lord warns us that if we do not discipline our sons and daughters, they "will die for lack of discipline, led astray by {*their*} own folly" (Proverbs 5:23). Clearly, we don't want our kids to be led astray or die. Therefore, we must not take disciplining them lightly.

> *Without discipline, your kids will be led astray and come to ruin. Don't take it lightly.*

The Lord refines us through discipline so we can be blessed and be a blessing. And through appropriate discipline, we have the opportunity to receive wisdom. As Billy Graham has said, "God does not discipline us to subdue us, but to condition us for a life of usefulness and blessedness."[2]

This should be your same motivation regarding your children. Without discipline, they will be brought to ruin because of the choices that result from that lifestyle. With discipline, they will be prepared and positioned to be blessed and be a blessing.

In summary, don't "lose heart" when your children are not fond of your discipline. Press through their resistance and understand that it may be painful for both the disciplined as well as the discipliner. In the end—after you have given good, effective discipline—you and your children will enjoy a harvest of righteousness and peace. Indeed, discipline is good for us and for those we love.

A Lesson in Discipline, Straight from the Horse's Buck
How Alan Learned Not to Take His Bad Mood Out on Others

It amazes me how two children raised in the same environment can be so different from each other. Stephanie absolutely loved horses. It was love at first sight. As a baby she would hold up her little arms for me to pick her up and hold her on the horse. She loved riding them, grooming them, everything.

Alan, on the other hand, loved playing any game as long as it included some kind of ball. In fact, when he was little, he would sleep with a ball and his "banky" when he got in his crib. Although he grew up with horses, he really didn't want anything to do with them, except on a few occasions—like when we took the horses out west for a ride, and during his teen years when he met girls who loved horses. So we constantly had one child playing catch and the other on a horse.

As stated earlier, good discipline *trains*. There may be pain involved, but it is temporary. On one occasion in my son's life, that discipline came from a pony. After several warnings from myself and Lady, our son learned an important lesson.

I will never forget the time Alan came home from a hard day in fifth grade. He seemed quite angry, so I tried to talk to him.

"What's wrong, Alan?" I said.

"Nothing!" he muttered as he began to walk down to the barn. Curious, I followed him there It had been so long since he voluntarily went to see the horses. I knew something was up.

"Where are you going?" I asked.

131

"Nowhere!" he said as he continued toward Lady's stall. Without saying a word, I watched him fumble with her halter as he tried to remember how it went on. She stood patiently as he pulled one strap over her head and then the other, only to realize he had put her nose in the wrong piece. Once he finally got it on, he led her out of the stall and tied her up.

"What are you going to do?" I questioned.

"Ride!" came his brief explanation. He found the bridle, and after several unsuccessful attempts to get the bit in her mouth, he asked for some help.

"Do you want her saddle?" I asked.

"Nope." He grunted. "I'm gonna ride her bareback." I found that answer interesting and amusing, but I said nothing.

He found the step stool, hopped on Lady's back, and gave her a hard kick in her sides. Surprised by the sharp kick, Lady bolted forward, obeying his command. Suddenly, Alan lost his grip and almost slid off. Regaining himself, he yelled, "Stupid horse." He then yanked her reins to the right to move her up toward the house.

By now, I was not enjoying watching Alan take out his bad mood on Lady. So I stopped him and said, "Alan, I don't know what is going on inside of you, but I do know it is not Lady's fault! Don't treat her as though it is!"

"I'm fine Mom," he retorted. "I'm not doing anything wrong. I just want to ride."

As he rode her up to the house, I could tell Lady was just as confused as me. She really was trying to do what was being asked of her, but he was still asking her in a rough manner. I warned him again, "You need to treat her with respect. She does not deserve being handled roughly. She is being patient, but I can't promise you she will continue."

Alan shot me a glaring look and gave Lady a swift kick in the direction he wanted to go. At that moment, I realized two things. One, he was not listening to me, and two, I had a couple of options as to how to handle it. I could either pull him off Lady myself, or I could let her handle it. By now, I knew her quite well and what she was and was not capable of. She had taken care of our kids for many years, and I had put their lives in her hands as she carried them over mountains, through rivers, and in horse shows.

As Alan continued his yanking and kicking, I noticed that Lady was now giving her own warnings. She was pinning her ears back, swishing her tail, and tossing her head. One last warning from me and multiple warnings from Lady were still not taken seriously by my angry boy.

Finally, she did it. She had tried to obey his orders and had warned him to calm down, and now she had had enough. With one solid buck, she put Alan on the ground. Thankfully, the only thing that was injured was his pride.

No discipline or words could have taught my son more than what Lady taught him in the matter of a few minutes. Don't take your bad mood out on somebody else or they may put you on your keister!

Endnotes

[1]Quotes on *Children and Family* (http://dailychristianquote.com/dcqfamily.html, accessed 10/5/13).
[2]Quotes on *Discipline* (http://dailychristianquote.com/dcqdiscipline.html, accessed 10/5/13).

Reflection and Application

1. Do you consistently discipline your children? If not, why? What is holding you back? If you do discipline your children, what is motivating your efforts? Is there anything the Holy Spirit is prompting you to change after reading this chapter?

   _____

   _____

   _____

2. God wants your discipline to be planned and thought out. What unacceptable behaviors or attitudes do you frequently see in your kids that need to be corrected? Jot them down. Do you have a plan of action to discipline them in these areas? If so, describe it. If not, take a moment to pray and ask God for His wisdom. Write what He reveals.

   My Child's Unacceptable Behavior   **My Plan of Discipline to Train Them**

   _____   _____

   _____   _____

   _____   _____

   _____   _____

   _____   _____

   _____   _____

   For questions 1 and 2, take a few moments to pray. Get God involved by asking Him for wisdom to see the things you need to see and do what you can to bring about positive change.

3. Good, effective discipline produces good results. Stop and think. What good results have come forth from your discipline? What good qualities can you see in your children? How did you discipline them to achieve this? What can you learn from these situations and apply in areas where they presently need discipline?

   _____

   _____

   _____

"Most confusion over how to discipline results from parents' failure to define the limits properly. If you're hazy on what is acceptable and unacceptable, then your child will be doubly confused. Therefore, don't punish until you have drawn the boundaries too clearly to be missed. Most children will then accept them with only an occasional indiscretion."

—**Dr. James Dobson**[1]

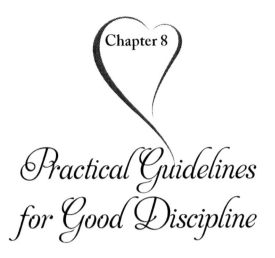

Chapter 8

Practical Guidelines for Good Discipline

*If you refuse to discipline your son, it proves you don't love him;
for if you love him, you will be prompt to punish him.*
Proverbs 13:24 TLB

As we have learned, without rules kids will become rebellious. Rules are the discipline needed to guide them safely down the highway of life. There is bad discipline and there is good discipline. In this chapter we will cover six major guidelines for good discipline, including the importance of disciplining in love, staying in control, and why consistency is so vital. We will also talk about some practical advice for parenting older kids.

BEGIN IN LOVE…
STAY IN CONTROL

Without question, your discipline is better understood and received when you administer it *in love and in control*. If your child does something wrong and you explode and begin yelling at them, they will tend to focus more on your emotional meltdown and less on what they did wrong. Ranting and raving uncontrollably only serves to deafen your children to the voice of correction and training they need to hear.

Think about this. Let's say you are at work, and your boss called you into his office because you violated a company policy. If he begins yelling at you and attacking your character, what do you think your response would be? If he said, "I can't believe you were so stupid as to pull a trick like that!" how would you react?

There is a good chance you would begin to cower as you watched his face turn various shades of red. You would also more than likely lose a lot of respect for him if he treated you that way. Where would your focus be—on your actions or his emotions? In the same way, when you yell and lose control while correcting your children, they become fearful and lose respect for you. Not only are you not respecting them but you are also not respecting yourself. You are out of control and everyone in earshot knows it!

Therefore, discipline must be administered in love and in control. If your child's unacceptable behavior is sending your blood pressure through the roof, press pause on the situation. If you are at home, send them to their room to give yourself time to calm down and think clearly. If you are out, take two or three deep breaths, and calmly but firmly advise them that they will be dealt with appropriately when you return home.

In both cases, you are remaining in control of your emotions and giving yourself time to calm down and discipline your child in love, not anger. That is the important key during any discipline moment. You want to convey that their action does not negate the love that you have for them. You are disciplining them because of the poor choice they made. You love them so much that you are willing to discipline them so that they can mature and prosper from your instruction and love!

> *Discipline must be administered in love and in control in order to be heard and received.*

END IN LOVE AND RESTORATION

As your children get older, it is important to make sure they know *why* they are being disciplined. While correction for some unacceptable behavior is obvious, other lessons are not as clear. When appropriate, explain to them what they did wrong and why they earned the consequences. To ensure that they understand, have them repeat what you explained. This not only helps them change the behavior, it also teaches them vital skills of communication and conflict resolution that they will take with them the rest of their lives.

Once you have given them the appropriate discipline and know they understand, have *a time of restoration.* Tell them you love them and believe in them. Follow this up with a big hug. This assures them of your unconditional love and keeps your heart connected to theirs. Many times after receiving discipline, the child will be the one to initiate the hug.

I still remember the first time that happened with our son Alan. He had been disrespectful enough to earn a spanking. I wanted to administer it in a loving way, so we sat down together to make sure he understood why he was being corrected. Until then, I had not spanked him. But in that moment I quickly realized that what my parents used to tell me was right. It really did "hurt me as much as it hurt him."

After I administered two or three swats on his well-padded bottom, I said, "I hope you have learned an important lesson through this." He wrapped his arms around me and said, "I love you, mom." I had read of that kind of response in a book, but I had never experienced it personally. He truly had learned his lesson, and restoration was completed.

I hugged him back and gave him a word of encouragement about himself. "Alan, you are a good boy, and I believe you're capable of not being that disrespectful again." Like a sponge, he absorbed my words, and life quickly resumed as though there had been no incident.

So always remember to end your time of discipline in love and restoration. There should always be a beginning and an end. If you put your child in a corner for a time out, set a timer. When it is over, express your love to them through words and affection. Tell them that you believe they are very capable of doing what they are supposed to do. Give them a big hug and move forward. Do not hold a grudge against them. Instead, show them as much love as you did before the discipline. Your love and affection confirms that the correction has ended and it is time to move on.

Always end your time of discipline in love and restoration. Tell them you love them and believe in them, and follow it up with a big hug.

BE CONSISTENT

Along with administering your discipline in love, *consistency* is very important. The rules of your home should be the same yesterday, today, and tomorrow. Consistency creates stability. It provides structure and security for your children that they crave but many times aren't aware of. The key to staying consistent is learning to plan ahead. It is knowing how you want to train your child and what rules you expect them to follow.

Again, consider the example of the boss who calls you into his office for breaking a company policy. Let's say the company rule is that no one is to leave the workplace before 5:00 p.m., but it is acceptable to leave at 4:30 p.m. if your work is done. That being understood, you completed your work early the previous Friday and left at 4:30 p.m. Then on Monday, you came into work and were reprimanded because you left before 5:00 p.m. You are sent home the next day without pay and are now labeled a troublemaker. How confusing and frustrating would that be?

To ensure that you comply with company policy, you stay until 5:00 p.m. from then on. Two weeks later you get called into the boss' office again. This time, you are reprimanded because you were supposed to stay until 6:00 p.m.! Apparently, the rules had changed, but they failed to inform you. How would this situation make you feel? Would you have a lot of trust or respect for the company? Would you want to keep working there? I don't believe I would.

What you would learn is that the rules are inconsistent, and there is no way to know what is acceptable or unacceptable. Without consistent rules, you are left with little more than a guessing game, not to mention a growing desire to leave. The same is true for your children when you don't consistently enforce the rules or the rules are always changing.

The key to staying consistent is learning to plan ahead. It is knowing how you want to train your child and what rules you expect them to follow.

INCONSISTENCY CAUSES INSTABILITY.

Let's look at this in light of a parenting situation. Imagine you have discussed with your child what disrespect is in your home. You have told them it is important for them to be respectful, and if they are not, a punishment will follow. The rule has been explained, and they understand it.

The first time they break the rule, you enforce it and issue a punishment. But a week later when they break the rule a second time, you choose not to discipline them. You had a long, tiring day at work, and you really don't want to spend your time correcting them and sending them to their room. In fact, you would like to just enjoy their company and have a nice evening watching a favorite family movie. So, you make the decision to not enforce the rule.

What did your child learn from your inconsistency? They learned that your words and rules don't really matter. With that in mind, they become disrespectful the next day. But by then, you are well-rested and ready for battle. You may begin to think to yourself, *I can't believe he is treating me this way. He knows better. Now, he is going to get it!* Immediately, you issue a punishment in anger. Your child becomes frustrated and confused. And instead of learning that it is inappropriate to treat others disrespectfully, their focus is on you and your out-of-control emotions.

Inconsistency creates instability in your child's life, allowing rebellion and bitterness to take root. How can you avoid this dangerous snare?

LET YOUR YES BE YES AND YOUR NO, NO!

Jesus gives us a powerful principle to live in Matthew 5:37. He says, "Let your Yes be simply Yes, and your No be simply No..." (AMP). In other words, if you tell your children you are going to do something, *do it.* Let your word be your bond. If you promise to throw a chair out the window if they "ever do that again," be prepared to throw a chair. If you don't intend to do something, don't say it.

This reminds me of a seven-year-old boy I knew named Blake. By most people's standards, Blake would be considered a strong-willed child. He knows what he wants in life and believes his desires are worth fighting for.

> *If you tell your children you are going to do something, do it. Let your word be your bond.*

On one particular occasion, Blake asked his parents to take him to McDonald's for lunch. Kindly but firmly, they responded, "No, we are going to have lunch at home."

Deciding this was a battle he was ready to fight, Blake began to cry, "But I want McDonald's." His parents tried to ignore his pleas, but he only became more adamant. "I want to go to McDonalds *now!*"

Hoping he did not hear what they said, Blake's parents tell him again, "No, we are going to have lunch at home."

Blake now escalates all the louder, "No! I want to eat *now*, and I want to go to McDonald's!"

Clearly, Blake has asked his parents for a fight. The deep-seated issue is not so much that he wants to go to McDonald's. The heart of the battle is wrapped around two questions: *Who is in control* and *who is going to win*. For most children, this is the foundation for the fight. They want their own way and they want to be in control.

As a parent, you must remember the reasons for the battle and answer these questions in no uncertain terms. Your answer must be consistent and the message must be clear: "I am in control, and you are not going to have your way!" Through your attitude, actions, and words, you must convey this message. In the case of Blake's parents, they need to convey:

> "Our words mean something, Blake. *No* means *no*. We are in control, not you. We love you so much that we are willing to engage you in this battle, but you will not win regardless of how much you protest. We are in control, and we have no need to yell at or threaten you because our words mean what they say. If you continue in this battle, we are willing and more than able to issue appropriate discipline to help you understand. It will be just the thing you need to help you be a secure, happy child. You can trust us and our words."

This is what it means to *let your yes be yes and your no be no*.

> *Through your attitude, actions, and words, you must convey that you are in control and your children are not going to have their way.*

FOLLOW THROUGH.

Once you promise a particular consequence for a particular behavior, you must follow through. If you say you are going to take away your child's phone for the week, then take their phone. This communicates that your yes is still yes and your no is still no. The same holds true for a promise you made to do something with or for them. For instance, if you say you are going to attend their dance recital, then be at their dance recital.

Idle threats and promises show a weakness in your parenting. They are out-of-control responses that are as useless as the breath it takes to speak them. Children quickly learn to recognize a lack of follow through and will utilize it to their advantage every chance they get.

Such was the case with "Josh," a ten-year-old boy I observed while standing in line at an amusement park. He and his mom were having a conversation that I and many others easily overheard. He was pushing her to buy him a toy he saw at the park. Firmly, his mom replied, "It costs too much, son. I'm not going to buy it."

At this, Josh began making a scene in the line, and his mom was at her wits' end. To counter his theatrics, she began threatening him. "If you don't shut up about the toy, I'm going to take you out to the car and make you sit there for the rest of the day while everyone else is having fun."

Josh was not fazed. He was not going to be deterred from his battle. He and his mom both knew that she was not going to have him sit in the car on a 95-degree day, not to mention they were frozen in line with the rest of us. Determined to get his way, Josh continued to make his demands, and his mom continued with her threats. Her words meant nothing, and they both knew it. They were an empty, idle threat. I imagine this was their way of life. He knew he could push her limits until she finally gave in, and that is exactly what he did.

The bottom line: Don't make idle threats or promises. Say what you mean, and mean what you say. Let your yes be yes and your no be no. Threats without action go in one ear and out the other. If you find yourself making idle threats or promises, stop and ask yourself, *Is this working in my child's life?* If it is not, why not make some changes? When a challenging opportunity for discipline arises, pause and pray. Ask God what you should say and then say it with confidence. As the Bible instructs, "…Everyone should be quick to listen, slow to speak, and should not get angry easily" (James 1:19 GW).

> *Don't make idle threats or promises.*
> *Let your yes be yes and your no be no.*

GIVE YOUR KIDS AGE-APPROPRIATE, TAILOR-MADE DISCIPLINE

Another important guideline to consider regarding the kind of discipline you administer is to make sure the punishment is *age-appropriate*. I heard a story about a father who was abusive. He ran a lumber company and often had his boys help out. The youngest was six years old, and if he did something his father deemed wrong, he ordered the little boy to unload the logs from the truck. That is *not* age-appropriate! That is abusive.

I heard of a mother who had a four-year-old girl who accidentally spilled her milk. The mother felt that it was worth punishing, so she made the little girl scrub the entire kitchen floor. Again, that is not age-appropriate! It is abusive, and spilling milk on accident is not a punishable offense.

Let the punishment fit the crime. Spanking a child because he or she forgot to feed "Fluffy" does not fit the crime. Neither does telling Johnny to "meditate" for an hour as to why he stole a car. The level of punishment needs to match the level of disobedience. That is what I mean by let the punishment fit the crime. At the same time, it should also be age-appropriate. The discipline you give should be something that will serve as a reminder why they should not repeat that behavior in the future.

Proverbs 13:13 says, "He who scorns instruction will pay for it, but he who respects a command is rewarded." Begin to ask yourself, what discipline does this child need that will help him respect a command?

Unlike a hat or a wristwatch, your discipline should *not* take a "one-size-fits-all" approach. It should be tailor-made. Each child is unique, and while many discipline principles are universal, their application is not. So as you consider your child's age, you must also take into account their personality.

For instance, a child who likes time alone could care less about being placed in the corner. It just gives him a chance to see how many bricks it takes to create his height. A swat on the seat of his pants might be just the thing he needs to adjust his behavior. It could be the thing he dreads most. His sibling, on the other hand, could care less about a swat. To him it is a quick and easy punishment, allowing him to go about his business. But put him in the corner and he believes the world has ended. It is the punishment he dreads most; it is what I call his "Achilles heel."

Let the punishment fit the crime. The level of discipline given needs to match the level of disobedience.

UNDERSTAND AND APPLY THEIR ACHILLES' HEEL

Achilles was a warrior in Greek mythology. He was the son of the sea nymph, Thetis. Legend says that when it was prophesied that Achilles would die in the Trojan War, Thetis tried to protect him by rubbing him with ambrosia to make him immortal. She then bathed him in the River Styx. The waters made him invulnerable, except for the heel by which his mother held him while bathing him in the river. Thus, the term Achilles' heel refers to someone's key weakness.

Each of your children has an Achilles' heel. And when discussing discipline, you want to find out what it is in order to use their weakness to develop their strength.

David, for instance, loves video games and plays them every chance he gets. When he comes home from school, he is supposed to do his homework and chores first before he plays any games. That's the rule, and he knows it. But there are times when he chooses to ignore the rule. He lies to his parents and says he is staying after school to study, but then goes to a friend's to play video games.

Perhaps David's sneaky behavior would call for using his Achilles' heel—taking away his video game privileges. Applying this punishment for a period of time will cause him anguish and likely deter him from lying to his parents and not doing what he is supposed to do first.

That being said, you don't want to overuse your child's Achilles' heel. You want to save it for their "big offenses," helping to discipline them in the areas of their greatest need. If you use it every time they do something wrong, that "heel" will become numb and ineffective. For example, if your child's Achilles' heel is a spanking and they are spanked every time they do something wrong, they will begin to resent you. Moreover, the spanking will become worthless.

I encourage you to make a list of each of your children's common offenses. Along with it, make a list of punishment options. Match each offense with the appropriate disciplinary action—keeping in mind which punishment seems to be most effective with each child. If your child disobeys the rule, implement the decided-upon discipline that you believe will be most helpful for them to make better choices in the future.

By using your child's key weakness—their Achilles' heel—you can develop their strength in key areas.

BE ON THE SAME PAGE

Deciding on the appropriate discipline can create a lot of dissension in the home and be stressful on a marriage—especially when parents have differing views. One exercise I give moms and dads (and caregivers) in counseling is this: Plan a time when you can go out for coffee or dessert to discuss appropriate discipline options for each child—a time when you are not in the middle of a disciplinary conflict. Take a pen and notepad and list what you believe should be punishable offenses in your home along with age-appropriate discipline options. The goal of this exercise is to come to an agreement as to what are punishable offenses and how they should be handled.

With some offenses, you may need to be more specific. For instance, if you think being disrespectful is a punishable offense, define what constitutes disrespect in your home. Is it rolling the eyes or huffing and puffing when asked to do a chore? Or is it only words that are considered disrespectful? Next, categorize what you consider to be "big offenses" from those that are smaller. Both need to be addressed, but big offenses will require a stronger consequence. For instance, how do you discipline a child if he fails to do his chores or lies to you about where he is? Should these two deeds be treated the same? Discuss what disciplinary action should be taken for each offense. If there is an issue you cannot come to an agreement on, seek help from other people or sources that you both respect.

At this point, you have created a unified front. Both you and your spouse are *on the same page* and know what is considered unacceptable behavior and how to discipline it appropriately. You should review your plan periodically to see if it is working or if anything needs to be changed. Once you and your spouse are on the same page, you can inform your children of the rules and what is considered acceptable and unacceptable behavior. You may even want to post these "House Rules" in a high-traffic area of you home. Children need to know the rules, but they do not necessarily need to know all the consequences for breaking them.

Being on the same page will help drastically reduce the stress level in your parenting.

SOME ADDITIONAL ADVICE
FOR DEALING WITH OLDER KIDS
Make Sure You Get Something Out of It.

I realize you may be dealing with older children, so I want to offer a few additional specific tips in this area. First of all, make sure that when you administer discipline you are not being punished too! If you are going to take the time to punish your child, make sure you get something out of it. For instance, if you decide to ground your son or daughter all weekend, don't get stuck watching them talk to their friends on the phone or play video games. Take away these privileges and give them something constructive to do—something that is going to benefit you and the rest of the family.

> *When disciplining your kids, give them something constructive to do that benefits you and the rest of the family.*

One weekend many years ago, Stephanie was "acting out" and insisting on getting her way. After attempting to reason with her, I quickly realized that it was not going to work. As her disrespect continued, I calmly but firmly announced, "There is a bathroom in the house that just got assigned to you for cleaning."

Choosing to ignore my announcement, she continued to engage in the battle. "But mom...."

Immediately, I declared, "We also have a second bathroom that will need cleaning once you finish the first one." With that, she shut her mouth.

At that point, her brother Alan chimed in. Thinking he was free and clear of punishment since we had just run out of bathrooms, he decided to follow suit and act the same way as Stephanie. But I would not let him get away with it. When it was all said and done, I ended up getting my entire house cleaned!

The next time I detected another disrespectful conversation about to happen, I reminded them of the bathroom. "Is it going to get cleaned, or is there a more respectful way you can choose to behave?" The choice was theirs: Be respectful or clean a bathroom. I shared this experience with one client who smiled at the suggestion. He had seven bathrooms in his house!

If your child is already assigned household responsibilities, the punishment should be a chore that is in addition to what he or she is already doing. This type of discipline kills two birds with one stone. One, they are serving time, and two, they are getting the opportunity to be trained in a skill they will need in the future.

Chores Must Be Done or They Can't Go.

From time to time, I have parents ask me, "What do I do when my child is supposed to clean the dishes, but they mess around and don't get them done? Then, when it is time for them to go out for the evening, I get stuck with the dishes."

The answer is very simple: If their chores are not done, they can't go. If they are asked to do the dishes "now," then that is when they are supposed to do them. If you have explained your request and they understood it, then that is what is expected. There are no misunderstandings. They know they have plans for the evening, and they know they have to do the dishes. If they are not done when their friends show up at the door, they can't go until the dishes are finished.

There is no need for you to nag, yell, or beg. And no need for them to plead. The choice was: "Either I do the dishes now so I can be ready to go out with my friends. Or don't do the dishes now, and I can't go when I am supposed to." If they made the choice to play around and not work, they need to live with the consequences.

If your child's chores are not done and they had ample time to do them, they can't go until they are done.

Don't Discipline Your Kids Using Guilt.

In counseling sessions, I sometimes hear parents warn their children of terrible things that are going to happen if they don't change their ways. For example, some have said...

"I'm going to end up in the hospital if you don't start helping me around the house."

Or, "If you continue to misbehave, bad things are going to happen to your dad and me."

And, "I'm going to have anxiety attacks if you keep arguing with me."

Although these statements may be true, they are not appropriate reasons to give your children to get them to change their ways. They are really nothing more than guilt-ridden manipulation.

These warnings get old fast and are very ineffective to bring about obedience.

Instead of manipulation, try *motivation*. Once you have established the house rules, enforce them. If they disobey what they clearly know they are supposed to do, follow through with age-appropriate, tailor-made discipline. On the other hand, when they obey the rules, celebrate their success with words of praise! Praise is powerful and goes a long way to reinforce a heart of obedience. The same is true with giving them a reward that will mean something to them.

DON'T EXASPERATE YOUR CHILDREN BY UNJUST REQUIREMENTS OR UNDUE DISCIPLINE.

I have touched on this before, but I believe it is worth repeating. Ephesians 6:4 warns, "Fathers {*and mothers*}, do not exasperate your children; instead, bring them up in the training and instruction of the Lord." And in Colossians 3:21 we are given a similar command. Here God says, "Fathers {*and mothers*}, do not embitter your children, or they will become discouraged." Indeed, training up a child requires love, not embitterment or exasperation.

These two verses tell us not to provoke our children unfairly. In Ephesians 6:4, we are instructed not to exasperate our kids. The Oxford Dictionary gives two definitions for *exasperate*: "to irritate or annoy to an extreme degree," and "to increase the bitterness or severity." Instead of irritating, annoying, and causing your kids severe bitterness, you are to apply godly principles to their lives through training and instruction in the Lord. In other words, help them see a demonstration of God's love and principles in your home. There will be times they will require correction, but many times they will simply require love and encouragement.

> *Instead of manipulation, try motivation.*
> *When your kids obey the rules, celebrate their*
> *success with words of praise!*

For example, take the above situation involving the chore of doing the dishes. In this case, let's say "Sasha" has plans to go out with her friends, and it is her turn to pick up and clean the dishes after dinner. Her family, however, did not sit down to eat until much later than usual. Now, she is in a quandary. They are still eating, and she has a half hour before she needs to be ready to leave. If Sasha's parents idolize the rules and stick to them rigidly, they would say, "Sasha, a rule is a rule. You know it is your night to do the dishes, and we can't break that rule. You'll just have to be late." That would be exasperating to her.

On the other hand, if her parents are training her in love, the conversation may go like this: "Sasha, we know you have a big event tonight, and we really got a late start with dinner. As soon as you are done eating, go ahead and get ready. We'll get the dishes. Do you need any help?"

This role models love and respect to Sasha, and it is life-giving to the parent-child relationship. It is saying, "Hey, we're with you. We're a team. How can we help?"

A week later, the tables are turned. Sasha's mom has an important meeting at the house, and once again dinner is a little behind schedule. Frantically, she begins to scramble, trying to get dinner and the house ready. She looks in the mirror and is frightened by what she sees. "They'll be here in a half hour," she cries. "Oh, no! Look at me!"

Sasha and the rest of the family look around the room and at each other. Sasha says, "Okay, mom needs help." Sasha politely shoves her mom into the bathroom and turns on the curling iron. Dad quickly loads the dishes in the dishwasher as Sasha returns to begin vacuuming. Teamwork! Love and respect were modeled and planted in Sasha, and love and respect were given back. That is the mark of good discipline and good parenting.

Friend, I encourage you to "Discipline your children while they are young enough to learn…" (Proverbs 19:18 GNT). By providing them with good discipline, you protect them from destruction and position them for great blessing!

Endnotes

[1] Dr. James Dobson, *The Strong-Willed Child* (Wheaton, IL: Living Books, Tyndale House Publishers, Inc., 1985) p.88.

Reflection and Application

1. Your discipline is best given *in love* and *in control.* Likewise, it is also important to *end in love and restoration* and *be consistent.* In your own words, briefly **explain the value** of implementing these parenting principles in your home.

   Discipline in Love and in Control

   _____

   _____

   _____

   End in Love and Restoration

   _____

   _____

   _____

   Be Consistent in Discipline

   _____

   _____

   _____

2. The punishment your child dreads most is his "Achilles' heel." Think for a moment. What would you say is your child's most dreaded punishment? (What he dreads most is likely linked to what he enjoys most.) What area(s) of greatest need can you apply his Achilles heel?

   _____

   _____

   _____

3. Of all the practical principles presented in this chapter, which one(s) stands out as the most important for you and your children at this time in your lives? Explain why. What can you do to more effectively apply this in your parenting?

   _____

   _____

   _____

For questions 1 to 3, take a few moments to pray and ask God for His wisdom to see the things you need to see and do what you can to bring about positive change.

"The only real qualification that parents need is a sincere and diligent desire to follow God's ways. God knew your strengths and weaknesses when you signed up to be a parent, and He still hired you. So if He doesn't regret giving you the job of raising His children, then you have nothing to feel guilty about. You are free to be yourself. You know your kids and what they need, so trust the insight God has given you."

—**Lisa Whelchel**[1]

Chapter 9

Striving for Excellence, Not Perfection — "Amanda's Story"

"If you wait for perfect conditions,
you will never get anything done."
Ecclesiastes 11:4 TLB

I watched as Amanda slumped into the chair, her eyes fixed on her shoes as the tears began streaming down her face. "I'm a failure," she moaned. "I'm not worthy of all the blessings the Lord has given me. I just can't do anything right."

The "presenting problem" was given to me by her concerned parents. They had come in for counseling the week before, exhibiting the same posture as their daughter. Amanda's dad was the CEO of a large corporation, and her mother was a stay-at-home mom. They had other children; Amanda was their oldest. All of them were home-schooled initially, and then they were sent to the best private schools in the area. With downcast eyes, Amanda's parents shared her story.

"Amanda is a very loving, compliant child who strives to do well in everything she does," they said. "Through her high school years, she has managed to maintain a 4.0 average. That is until she got a "B" in math last semester. That devastated her. She loves music, plays the piano for church, and is in concert choir. She also has excelled in dance and drama and was the star in the school play last spring. However, when she tried out for an upcoming production this fall, she was not offered the lead, but was asked to be an extra in the cast of characters. This was another devastating blow!"

Indeed, Amanda was not doing very well. A concerned friend had contacted Amada's parents and told them she was cutting herself in the school bathroom between classes. She was also anorexic. Apparently when no one was looking, Amanda was throwing her food away and wearing baggy clothes to hide all the weight she had lost. Her friend had found a poem Amanda had written about cutting herself to numb the pain she was feeling. When she showed it to Amanda's parents, they were devastated and guilt-ridden. They loved her deeply and only wanted the best for her.

"How could this happen?" they cried. "Amanda has everything. She is super smart and has so many gifts and talents. We know the Lord has great plans for her, and if she applies herself, she will be right back at the top of her class again. Why would she do this?"

"...From now on we estimate and regard no one
from a [purely] human point of view
[in terms of natural standards of value]...."
—2 Corinthians 5:16 AMP

How Do Children Like Amanda Think?

"Why?" That is the question that haunts parents who are faced with this type of crisis. What I have found is that children like Amanda are sincerely confused. They cannot settle for anything less than *perfection*. Amanda had to be the best in everything. If she was not, she saw herself as a failure. Her identity had become inseparably linked to her performance. In her mind, anything less than perfect conveyed that she was a disappointment to her parents, teachers, friends, and herself. Others were allowed to have short falls, but not her.

Children like Amanda struggle because they don't understand the difference between perfectionism and excellence. As a result, they set themselves up for failure. In their minds, healthy, "hope to" goals become "have to" goals. This demanding mindset tends to bleed over into their relationships with parents, family, and friends, and they associate receiving love with performance.

In their minds, love comes with a price tag—it must be earned. The better they perform, the more they are loved. "If I get straight 'A's in school," they think, "my parents will love me more. And if I get first chair in the orchestra, my teacher will admire me more." For perfectionistic kids, unconditional love is a foreign concept that flies in the face of their way of thinking.

If Amanda continues to hold a perfectionistic mindset, she may never try out for another school play for fear of not getting the lead role. She may also avoid taking any more math classes for fear that she is not good at math. I have seen children and teens only take on a sport, hobby, or class if they felt guaranteed that they would be highly successful. They just were not willing to take any risks.

In the mind of a perfectionist, love must be earned.
The better they perform, the more they are loved.

As a counselor, I am always curious to see where this ideology originated. In some cases, it comes from the child's parents who are perfectionists themselves. They are high achievers and understand how hard work can produce great results. In their hearts, they want the very best for their children. While nothing is wrong with wanting the best, this desire can be quite devastating if it is out of balance.

Many times, this perfection ideology comes from within the child. It is actually connected with the way they are wired. Through their own introspection, they begin to realize that no one is expecting these things from them except themselves. They have become their own worst enemy. This is where knowing your child's heart becomes so important.

As I said, perfectionistic kids like Amanda struggle to understand and receive unconditional love. They have mistakenly gotten the idea that receiving love is a direct result of their performance. The better they perform, the more they are loved and accepted. They feel they have to *earn* it. But as we have learned in an earlier chapter, love that is earned is conditional. Unconditional love is unearned—it is from God Himself and is guaranteed without conditions or limitations. This powerful resource is available to all who are believers in Christ!

"When someone becomes a Christian, he becomes
a brand new person inside. He is not the same
anymore. A new life has begun!"
—2 Corinthians 5:17 TLB

God's Grace Is Amazing!

As I strive to get to the heart of these children and teens in counseling, I often ask them what their expectations are for themselves. Clearly, their expectation bar is very high, and for them, reaching it is not an option—it is a mandate. Interestingly, when I ask them if their high expectations are in line with what the Lord expects, many adamantly shake their heads and reply, "Yes." They then recite the verse in which Jesus says, "Be perfect, therefore, as your heavenly Father is perfect" (Matthew 5:48). But in light of this verse's original meaning, perfection as we know it is not what Jesus was implying.

God already knows that none of us are perfect. He knew that we could not live up to His standard of holiness outlined in the law. He knew that we would have bad thoughts, mess up our relationships, and covet and be envious of other people's things. He knew this not just about us, but also our kids. He knew that every day would not be their best. He knew that they would sometimes misbehave and get things wrong on a homework assignment. He knew they would sometimes not score a goal in the big game or get the lead in the school play. *He knows all things*, including our need for a Savior.

That is why He sent His Son, Jesus. He was fully God, yet fully man. By the life-giving power of God's Spirit, Jesus walked the earth and lived a sinless life. Oh, He was tempted in all the ways that we are, but He did *not* sin (see Hebrews 4:15). Being perfect, He became the perfect sacrifice to pay the penalty for our sin. In other words, He took our punishment for all the wrong things we have done or will ever do. Through faith in Him, we are set free from the punishment we deserve and from the pressure to live perfectly.

What is just as amazing is that when Jesus took our sin and punishment, He gave us His amazing *grace* in exchange. Grace is God's supernatural strength (power and ability) to do what we could never do on our own. In our imperfection, we cling to the One who is perfect. He gives us grace and the ability to grant grace to others. Through grace we also have the ability to forgive and love others. We become encouragers to those who are struggling because we have struggled too. We know what it is like not to be perfect. From the moment we invite Jesus into our lives until "death do us part," these qualities of God's grace are being "perfected" in us. Indeed, we are a work in progress!

> *Through faith in Jesus, we are given **grace**. And we are set free from the punishment we deserve and from the pressure to live perfectly.*

DOES THIS DESCRIBE YOUR CHILD?

To help your children truly be successful, you must understand their heart. Knowing their heart will reveal if they are self-motivated or need motivation from you. For instance, they may act as though they do not care about doing their homework. But is this a result of them being lazy and unmotivated, or is it because they are so focused on doing it perfectly that they are fearful of failing?

By being in relationship with your child and knowing their heart, you will be able to discern if their expectations of themselves are unrealistic and need to be challenged. If they are an over-achiever or perfectionist, they will need to be reminded often to simply do their best and not worry about the results. No one's perfect. Everyone has special talents and is uniquely gifted in certain areas—but not in *all* areas. That is not to say that you should discourage your child from trying something new, but rather encourage their efforts for excellence and not demand perfection.

I can still remember times when we rejoiced with our children over a "C" they earned in a class. They had done their best, and that was what mattered. Likewise, when they had the courage to try out for a sport for the first time, we were thrilled. Even if they didn't make the team, we were pleased that they tried. Excellence was their goal—not perfection. With each opportunity, they learned to rely on Christ to strengthen them to do their very best.

I encourage you to teach your children to pursue *excellence*, not perfection. While doing everything flawlessly is impossible, doing the best they can with what they have is not. This is *excellence*. Instill within their hearts the timeless principle of Philippians 4:13: "For I can do everything *through Christ*, who gives me strength" (NLT). With Christ's strength, they can demonstrate a godly attitude when they don't get the lead in the school play. They can walk with their head held high because their identity is in the One who made them and not in their performance.

> *Teach your children to pursue excellence,*
> *not perfection. Excellence is doing the best*
> *you can with what you have.*

Endnotes

[1]Lisa Whelchel, *Creative Correction* (Wheaton, IL: Tyndale House Publishers, 2005) p. 132.

Reflection and Application

1. Are there any aspects of Amanda's story that resonate with you personally? How about with one of your children? If so, which ones? How does her story help you see yourself and your child in a new light?

   "I can PERSONALLY identify with Amanda in that..."

   _____

   _____

   _____

   "My son/daughter _____ is similar to Amanda in that..."

   _____

2. As a believer in Jesus Christ, you are a brand new person inside, and your identity is in Him. The same is true for your children. Check out these verses from God's Word. Carefully read over each *alone* and then *with your child.* Then write down what God is speaking to you through them.

   1 Corinthians 5:17, 21; Colossians 3:3; Romans 8:35, 37; 2 Corinthians 2:14

   Through these verses, I believe God is showing me...

   _____

   _____

   _____

   Through these verses, _____, my child believes God is showing them...

   _____

   _____

3. From where does your child draw his or her worth and value? Is it from how well they do in school or sports? Is it from how well they behave? Or is their worth and value drawn from the unconditional love and acceptance of God? Take some time to sit with them and ask, "What makes you feel valuable? Loved? Accepted?" Listen to what they say and pray with them to know deep in their heart that their worth and value is in Christ.

   _____

   _____

   This would be a very good question for you to answer for yourself. Your worth and value come from Christ and Him alone.

Part IV:

Relationship Plus Rules Provide a Solid Foundation for Instruction

"Many fathers have never said the words 'I love you' to their children. You may be one of them. You think they know you love them, but if you don't tell them they can't be sure. Tell your kids you love them, then show it by sharing your life with them. Dad, turn your heart to your children. Don't let anything take precedence over them.

...Be a man of your word. When you make a promise, live by it. If you break a promise, go to your children and explain why you can't do what you said you'd do. ...The integrity of a father's word is a standard for the lives of his children. ...Dad, turn your heart to your children. Turn your heart to God."

—**Dave Roever**[1]

(Note: What is true for Dad is also true for Mom.)

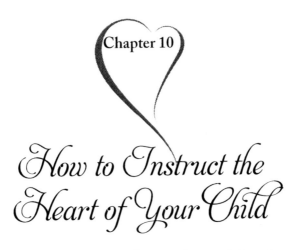

How to Instruct the Heart of Your Child

"The instructions of the Lord are perfect, reviving the soul.
The decrees of the Lord are trustworthy, making wise the simple."
Psalm 19:7 NLT

Remember the formula we discussed in chapter 2? Let's go over it again to refresh our memory: Relationship + Rules = Instruction. When you have a good Relationship with your child along with good Rules, you have a solid foundation for good Instruction. By role modeling your values and providing them with consistent, loving discipline, your child will give you a *passport* to instruct them.

The greatest benefit of giving your child godly instruction is that it will guide them throughout their life. The Bible confirms this saying, "Son, do what your father tells you and never forget what your mother taught you. Keep their words with you always, locked in your heart. Their teaching will lead you when you travel, protect you at night, and advise you during the day. Their instructions are a shining light; their correction can teach you how to live" (Proverbs 6:20-23 GNT).

As a parent, life offers you ample opportunities to teach and build character in your child's life and mold him or her into a godly adult. Life lessons are all around you, and as you learn to recognize and utilize them, they will provide your child with instruction that will help determine the course of their future. I experienced this firsthand during my growing years.

> *A good Relationship with your child along with good Rules provides a solid foundation for good Instruction.*

LIFE LESSONS BY A RIVER

My parents took every opportunity to teach me about life. I am so grateful that they were not simply babysitters. I also praise God that I was raised before electronics captivated our lives. In my day, there were no iPods, computer games, Play Stations, or videos. Consequently, there was a lot more conversation—especially between my parents and me. And that conversation inevitably turned into opportunities to "train me up in the way I should go."

For us, camping was a wonderful time for bonding as a family and imparting life-changing instruction. That is why my husband and I carried on the tradition with our kids and recommend it to other families. Part of the fun of camping is in the preparation—especially packing the gear. When we looked at all the equipment it supposedly took for three people to "rough it," we were amazed that any of the early settlers were able to survive heading out west on horseback.

History romances the old west with painted pictures of a lone cowboy astride his horse, having all the essentials of life rolled up neatly on the back of his saddle. For months, he traversed over mountain ranges, crossed streams, braved the weather, and had all the comforts of home in that one roll. How he did it, I will never know.

When our family gathered together our "essentials," it amounted to several piles. To figure out how it would all fit into the back of our station wagon took an engineering degree. Yet, we were determined to rough it in luxury. Necessity being the mother of invention, we always seemed to find a way to fit everything we needed.

Take, for instance, our cooking gear. My dad had cleverly converted my old toy box into a portable kitchen equipped with a silverware drawer, place for pots and pans, a canned good section, and a sink. Precision was exact; there was no room for disorder. All items had to be placed in their designated space or they would not fit. As with many things, we worked together to design our "grub box" and carry out the challenging task of packing the station wagon.

Since camping is supposed to be fun, we made the work fun too. Clearing the site and gathering fuel for the fire was rewarding. But my favorite task was putting up the tent. My dad and I were always responsible for this. It became a game to beat the previous time of raising the tent.

Life lessons are all around. Learn to recognize and utilize them to give your child godly instruction.

During those days of camping, I learned many things, including how to appreciate nature and the stillness of a cool morning. Watching for wildlife as they came out in the evening was simply amazing. I learned how to canoe and enjoy the sounds that rapids make and how to hear God's still, small voice as I silently drifted through the deep. I learned how to respect wildlife and the earth's environment. I also learned that panicking in a thunderstorm that is threatening your tent does not help. Indeed, there was something about camping that gave me an inner confidence that I could survive in any rough situation if I needed to.

One evening as we were camping by the Jacks Fork River, my dad suggested that he and I take a walk. I can still remember strolling down that river trail to the rocky beach below where we sat and observed the rapids. For quite some time, we rested quietly and enjoyed the sounds of nature. Then my dad broke his silence and said, "Peggy, life is just like the river we canoed on today. At times it will be like still waters, and other times you will have rapids that you will need to carefully navigate. There will be times of peace, times of hard rowing, and times of turmoil. So, expect it and know that God will be with you through each journey you take on your river."

I have never forgotten that time with my dad or his very wise words. When things get hard and I know I am in the rapids, I remember that God will get me through. There are still waters ahead. All I need to do is trust and rest in Him. What a blessing a parent's words of instruction are!

CONNECT YOUR KIDS WITH GOD

In Proverbs 1:8-9 God says, "Listen, my son, to your father's instruction and do not forsake your mother's teaching. They will be a garland to grace your head and a chain to adorn your neck."

If you knew your children would leave your home with your instruction and teaching adorning their neck and embedded in their heart, would you not have a feeling of peace? If you knew your children were incorporating godly wisdom into their choices, would you not worry less about them? The truth is you *can* know this, and it comes from helping your kids connect with God in relationship.

As Christians, we want our children to understand how valued they are by the Lord. They need to know that He is real and He is the One who determines their value; it is not other people or even themselves. We also want them to know that they can trust Him and turn to Him when they are sad, hurt, or confused. He always has their best interest in mind and has a good plan for their lives. Jeremiah 29:11 confirms this saying, "'For I know the plans I have for you,' says the Lord. 'They are plans for good and not for disaster, to give you a future and a hope'" (NLT).

Helping to develop your child's relationship with God begins with teaching them His Word. It continues to be strengthened as you seize opportunities to talk and pray with them about the challenges they are facing. These are prime times for instruction and connection. The more you connect them with God during their times of need, the more they will think and desire to seek Him on their own as they get older. Passionately pursuing Him with all their heart, soul, and strength will come more naturally. It is your godly instruction that sets the stage for them to know and please the Lord.

Opportunities to talk and pray with your kids about the challenges they are facing are prime times for instruction and connection.

One of the first scriptures we talked about was Proverbs 22:6: "Train up a child in the way he should go, and when he is old he will not depart from it" (NKJV). So where do you want your children to go? Now is the time to instruct them using the communication and relationship tools presented in this book.

If you want your children to gain wisdom that will protect them through life and will be a garland around their head and a chain to adorn their neck, train them up in the ways of the Lord. Use life's lessons to teach; they are the best tool of all. Indeed, there is an abundance of freedom to grant your teenager when you know he or she has chosen for his own, God-given values and a passion to please the one true God. Your job as a parent becomes much easier.

MOVING CAN BE HARD...
GOING TO A NEW SCHOOL EVEN HARDER

A Life Lesson in Loving the Unlovely and Being Kind to Strangers

We used to call our daughter "Princess Stephanie." During the earlier years of her life, we lived in a small, rural community in Kearney, Missouri—a town not far from Kansas City. There on a ten-acre mini-ranch, she was surrounded by many friends who lived on ten-acre mini-ranches themselves. When she wasn't playing with the neighbors, she was attending our small church in town, learning about God and enjoying relationships there.

When it came time for her to begin Kindergarten, it was just another social event! Stephanie did not think about the normal fears of Kindergarten. Fears like, "Who will I play with?" or "Will the other children like me?" Instead, she approached Kindergarten with the attitude, "So many friends, and so little time!" Indeed, life was good in Kearney.

As life would have it, an opportunity presented itself that required us to relocate across the state to the city of St. Louis. As we began packing up our belongings to head east, Stephanie was under the assumption that life there would be the same in St. Louis as it was in Kearney. *Of course, everyone will love me*, she thought. *Third grade at my new school will be just as great as it was in Kearney, and life will be an adventure!*

In Steph's mind, the move was no big deal. All she seemed to think about was how many new friends she could acquire in the shortest time possible. As a parent, I was a little concerned. I knew that life would probably be different, but I didn't want to dash her spirit or confidence. *Who knows?* I thought. *Maybe she will actually waltz into her new school with her 'great expectations' and get them.* Little did we know what awaited.

179

THE KINGDOM BEGINS TO CRUMBLE

For the first few weeks, Stephanie regularly shared with me about the new girls she was meeting. All seemed well, and I felt a sense of relief. I realized that my precious daughter would not be the big hit that she expected, but she seemed to be accepted. And that is what was most important. I put aside my fears.

However, by the third week, things began to change. One day Stephanie got off the bus in tears. "Mom, those girls told me they decided they didn't like me anymore," she cried. "They took my pencil box and stole my pencils. And one of them called me 'rat face.'"

Our Princess was not in her castle anymore. In fact, the kingdoms in St. Louis were very different from those in Kearney. Evidently, the jokes that were hilarious in the third grade in Kearney were met with blank stares in St. Louis. While in Kearney, it was not unusual to discuss with your friends what your favorite cow or pony did that morning. In St. Louis, this conversation was met with anger. One girl actually shoved Stephanie when she shared her news. Apparently, she had never seen a pony before, and it really irritated her.

On hearing this, I became quite irritated—as irritated as a momma bear. A momma bear will protect her cubs any way she can, even attacking if necessary. Thus, the saying, "Don't mess with a momma bear's cubs!"

How dare they talk to my sweet baby that way! I said to myself. *What kind of parents would not teach their girls to be loving and caring? That's just absurd, and it has to stop!*"

As I listened to Stephanie's sobs, I tried to comfort her by saying, "Don't worry about those girls, Stephanie. They don't know what they're missing. Tomorrow is another day, and there are a lot of girls at your school who you can choose to be friends with!"

The following week, I looked out of our window and was shocked by what I saw. While my sweet little girl was playing with the neighborhood kids, she suddenly knocked one of the boys to the ground. She then grabbed her brother Alan's hand and marched through our front door. When I asked her what had happened, she explained, "That boy was picking on Alan. I told him that if he was going to pick on Alan, he would have to deal with me first!"

Ah, I thought. *A future mother bear in the making!*

ESTABLISHING A NEW IDENTITY

The months that ensued were quite challenging. For the first time in Stephanie's life, she was struggling to establish her identity. It seemed that the days of gentle love and care were gone. The comforting thought that "Jesus loves you, and so do I" was like a wonderful bubble that had been burst. It was replaced with a mindset of caution and fear toward other classmates. Her existence became more focused on survival than sharing Christ's love.

For the first time ever, I saw Stephanie's desire to go to school virtually disappear. She had always loved school and loved learning. She also loved her teachers and her classmates. But her new environment had changed all of that. She had even lost confidence in who she was as a person. My heart broke as I watched this transformation.

Sadly, the bullying continued. On the playground, a girl tried to choke her and then threw a backpack in her face. On the bus, someone removed her glasses and then pushed her to the floor while she was trying to retrieve them. Incidents like these resulted in one trip after another to the principal's office.

For years, we had taught our kids that a person's identity was not based on what they wore, but on who they were on the inside. However, in our new hostile environment, I found myself wanting to buy my kids all the "in-brand" clothes I could find. If wearing the hottest tennis shoes and jackets would help them, I was willing to buy them—anything to help them get established.

Time passed and we developed some new practices. Before going to school each day, we played music with messages declaring how special our kids were and how God had a great plan for their lives. We also began to pray for them to find good friends and asked God to be a "hedge of protection" around them from those who meant them harm. We even prayed for the kids who were being mean and saying hateful things. Clearly, they weren't receiving much love at home, so we prayed that God would intervene and express His love to them.

Along with special prayers and encouraging music, we taught Stephanie to stand strong and not budge when someone was trying to bully her. The Bible says, "God didn't give us a *cowardly* spirit but a spirit of power, love, and good judgment" (2 Timothy 1:7 GW). As parents, Don and I continually built her up. As we painstakingly sent her out the door, we reminded her of *who she was in Christ* and that she belonged to Him. At times it was very difficult. Nevertheless, God used the situation to build her character and confidence and draw her into a closer relationship with Himself—the One who had brought her to St. Louis.

That experience eventually taught Stephanie the importance of reaching out to other new students. It also helped her befriend those who sat by themselves in the lunch room and at church. She came to despise cliques because of her new sensitivity for those left out. She actually learned *who* she was and *whose* she was. She realized that she was valued and loved by her family and her newfound friends—a priceless lesson that continues to guide her in her adult life today.

Endnotes

[1] *Parenting: Successful Church Leaders Share Biblical Principles for Raising Kids in the Nineties*, Compiled and edited by Hal Donaldson & Kenneth M. Dobson (Sacramento, CA: Onward Books, Inc., 1993) pp. 16-21).

Reflection and Application

1. One of my greatest times to receive instruction from my parents was during family campouts. When I was relaxed and having a good time, I was very receptive. Looking at your children, what would you say are three prime times when they are most relaxed and receptive to learning?

   _____

   _____

   _____

   _____

2. How important is it to God that you share the real-life stories and principles of His Word with your children? Carefully read these passages of Scripture. What is God showing you through these? **Deuteronomy 6:5-9; 11:18-21; 31:13; Psalm 78:1-8; 2 Timothy 3:16-17**

   _____

   _____

   _____

   _____

3. Have your children ever had to deal with situations similar to what Stephanie and Alan experienced after moving and going to a new school? If so, briefly describe what happened? What practical ideas and principles can you draw from this real-life story and apply in your own children's lives?

   _____

   _____

   _____

"Not only do you need to forget trying to be a perfect parent, but you also need to forget having perfect children. If you judge your success by whether your children turn out perfectly, you'll be setting yourself up to fail, because it will never happen.

...I encourage you to get a new definition of success in the area of parenting. You can do no more than your best. You can control your actions, but ultimately, your children are in control of their own responses. So judge your parenting by these three criteria: The quality of your love for your children; the model you've been to them; and the appropriateness of your actions (and reactions) to them."

—John Maxwell[1]

Chapter 11

Practical Steps to Changing Your Parenting Style

"... God who began the good work within you will keep right on helping you grow in his grace until his task within you is finally finished on that day when Jesus Christ returns."
Philippians 1:6 TLB

*I*n chapter 3, we discussed the four basic parenting styles— three of which are unhealthy. These include the "P" or *Permissive* parent, the "L" or *Legalistic* parent, and the "M" or *Manipulative* parent. If you see yourself as a "P," "L," or "M" parent, it is not too late to make changes.

Ultimately, *Godly* parenting should be your goal. It yields the highest and best results for both you and your children. As you begin to understand the principles in this book, you must also make a decision to *apply* them in your parenting. If you are willing to make some changes and become intentional and consistent, God will empower you with His grace to be the parent your child needs. All you have to do is ask Him. He will help you make daily choices to reap the rewards of happy, healthy children of which you can be proud.

In this final chapter, I want to offer five keys to establishing a new game plan in your parenting. We will also touch on the importance and power of believing in your children and why it is vital to always remember that our season of parenting is not a long one.

If you're willing to make some changes and become intentional and consistent, God will empower you with His grace to be the parent your child needs.

FIVE KEYS TO ESTABLISHING A NEW GAME PLAN

Once you have made a decision and commitment to make some changes, there are a few key steps you need to take to ensure that your plan succeeds. They are each linked to informing your children that change is coming. Like any game, if the rules have been changed, it is only fair to inform all the players.

ONE
Have a Family Meeting.

The first step to establishing a new game plan in your parenting is to have a family meeting. To get your child or children's attention, announce that there will be a special gathering at a designated date and time. Tell them you cannot discuss what the meeting is about until then, but reiterate that it is important. The mystery will pique their curiosity, and they will begin to grasp that something big is about to take place.

One vital note of caution: Do not have the meeting until you have an agreed-upon plan with your spouse and are ready to implement it. In order to be successful, you must be on the same page regarding acceptable and unacceptable behavior, consequences, and rewards.

TWO
Start with a Confession and an Apology.

At the beginning of the meeting, you may want to start off with a confession and an apology. Several parents have told me they started their meeting in this way, and it was very effective. For example, they shared something like this with their kids:

> "We have asked you to come to this important meeting in order to confess to you that we have sinned against you. In our endeavor to love you, we have failed to show you our love because of our inconsistent discipline. There are times when we have told you 'no' but then turned around and said 'yes' to what you wanted to do. We have asked you to do something but then gotten lazy and didn't follow through to ensure it was done. We have yelled at you, threatened you, and even walked away in the middle of an argument. There have also been times when your mother (or father) and I have argued with each other because we did not agree upon an appropriate punishment. I'm sure that has caused you confusion and frustration at times. It is not an example of loving you, and we ask for your forgiveness." (*Feel free to adjust the wording so that it is age-appropriate for your children.*)

The last thing your children are probably expecting was a confession and an apology from their parents. As much as some children may feel the power, or upper hand, from this experience, it also puts them in a double bind. If they argue with your confession, they are actually saying you are great parents. If they don't argue with your confession, it means they agree with you.

The first step to establishing a new game plan in your parenting is to have a family meeting.

THREE
Bring the Lord into Your Relationship.

The third step to take is to welcome the Lord into your parent-child relationship(s). He is the perfect Father and will give you wisdom, strength, creativity, and everything else you need to handle every situation that arises. At your family meeting, you may want to say something like:

"In addition to our lack of consistency in our discipline, we also realize that by not being good parents to you, we are sinning against the Lord. He has put your souls under our care, and we are to submit to His Word and authority concerning you. He has given us a short amount of time to train you in the way that you should go, and He wants us to be diligent about it. We need His strength daily to be loving in our relationship and courageous in our discipline. From this day forward, we welcome the Lord's presence and power in all we do. We ask for your patience as we strive to be parents the Lord will approve of." (*Again, feel free to adjust the wording so that it is fits for your children.*)

What happens when you welcome Jesus? Look at this example from Scripture. "Zacchaeus came down and was glad to *welcome*

Jesus into his home" (Luke 19:6 GW). By welcoming Jesus, Zacchaeus' heart was changed for the better (see verse 8). "Then Jesus said to Zacchaeus, 'You and your family have been saved today...'" (Luke 19:9 GW). When you welcome Jesus into your relationship with your children, you welcome His life-changing, saving power!

FOUR
Open the Floor for Discussion.

At this point in your family meeting, you want to open the floor for open, honest discussion. This can be done by stating something like:

> "As I said before, I'm sure that we have caused you confusion and frustration at times as a result of our inconsistency. We want to hear your heart at this time. Please let us know how our inconsistency or lack of discipline has confused or hurt you so that we can apologize and ask for your forgiveness. We want the air to be clear and the slate clean."

Clearly, this is a very pivotal point. It is here that hearts often open and are laid out on the table. In some families, the children's feedback is more focused on the parents' arguing or yelling at them or at each other; this is what has caused the most hurt. If this is the case with your children, please hear their hearts. Apologize for hurting them, and don't defend yourself for using inappropriate attitudes or behavior. If you asked for their heart, don't get after them for sharing it with you. Your position of humility and honesty will go a long way to help heal and restore their wounded hearts and your relationship.

> *Welcome the Lord into your parent-child relationship(s). He will give you everything you need to handle every situation that arises.*

FIVE
Lay Out the New Ground Rules.

The fifth step and final phase of your family meeting is to lay out the new ground rules. This includes taking time to explain what *disrespect* means in your household and giving examples of it. You will also want to clearly define what you consider punishable offenses as well as the acceptable behavior you are looking for. Next, discuss the chores that are expected to be done by each child, and explain that consequences will occur if they are not. You do not necessarily need to say *what* each of the consequences will be. Just assure them that there will be consequences.

Again, these are the things you want to have planned out *before* you have your family meeting. After the meeting, you may want to consider typing up and printing out your house rules and posting them in the family room and kitchen. You may also want to post your child's list of chores in their bedroom. These will serve as gentle reminders of what is expected of them.

At the end of your meeting, ask your children if they have any questions about the new rules. You may even want to have them repeat the rules back to you to make sure they understand. Again, ask them for patience as you move forward. Tell them you may stumble at times and give in where you shouldn't. But you promise to stay the course, building a loving relationship and providing consistent, loving discipline.

If you have been a Permissive or Manipulative parent, you may be challenged significantly by your child because they expect to get what they want. My advice to you is to expect them not to appreciate the changes. I also encourage you to push through the battles. If you stay consistent, they will eventually learn that there is a "new sheriff in town" and comply with the rules.

In summary, I offer three simple words to empower you as a parent: *loving, consistent discipline*. If you are consistent in loving your child and applying discipline to their life, there is a greater probability of training them up grounded in God, confident in their own value, and knowing right from wrong.

> *I offer three simple words to empower you as a parent: loving, consistent discipline.*

BELIEVE IN YOUR CHILDREN

Along with developing a new game plan for your parenting, I encourage you to believe in your child (or teen). Deep within their heart, they desire to grow up, spread their wings, and fly away. That is the natural order of life. It is God's design. They want to experience life, make their own decisions, and be respected. These traits should be encouraged and nurtured.

By believing in your child even before they are able to believe in themselves, you help prepare and lead them to the next stage of growth in their life. Saying things like, "I believe in you _____ (insert their name). You are gifted and talented and are going to do great things. God is *for* you, and He is helping you grow more and more every day. I can't wait to see the good things He has for you and will do through you!"

193

Dr. James Dobson has a great illustration for this aspect of parenting. He compares it to a football coach preparing his players. Each day the coach is out on the field during practices, providing them with personal, hands-on training. When game time comes, the players use the skills they developed in practice to play the game for real. Now the coach walks the sidelines, encouraging and guiding his players, but is not actually a part of their game. At halftime, he brings them together in the locker room, encouraging and instructing them in specific ways. He then sends them back out on the field to finish their game.

In a way, that is what you do as a parent. When your children are young, you are with them on the practice field, providing personal, hands-on training every step of the way. You tell them what to expect in life and how to avoid some blows that can come their way. You teach them how to go toe to toe with their foe. As they get older, they enter the real game of life, and you can no longer be with them every step of the way. You encourage them and give them the tools and confidence they need, but you remain on the sidelines as they play their game.

Believing in your son or daughter includes instilling in them a "Can-Do" spirit. God says they "...*Can do* all things through Christ who strengthens..." them (Philippians 4:13). They have the God-given abilities to accomplish their goals. So instead of planting doubt in their minds, plant faith. Instead of saying, "Boy, I sure hope you are good enough to go to college," say "Any college would be honored to have you. Where do you think you are going to go?" Statements like these reinforce the fact that God has a *good plan* for their lives—a plan filled with hope (see Jeremiah 29:11). It prepares them for the things that could come their way and instills confidence in their ability to handle them before they arrive.

I remember a time when Stephanie was getting ready to start a new school year. She was excited, but a little apprehensive. One day, we hiked up our hill and sat together to watch our horses graze and our dog bask in the sun. "You are really going to enjoy school, Stephanie," I said, "and you're going to do very well." I then praised her for how mature she was to be ready to begin school. Those words infused new life and peace into her. And that's what your words of encouragement will do for your child!

> *Believing in your child includes instilling in them a "Can-Do" spirit. God says they Can Do all things through Christ who strengthens them.*

CHERISH THE TIME...
IT GOES BY FAST

My husband, Don, and I fully enjoyed watching our kids grow and cherished each year we had with them. We laughed together, played together, and cried together. We enjoyed being a part of their activities and valued their thoughts and opinions on life. Now, Stephanie and Alan are grown and out on their own. We are empty nesters and our house seems so quiet. Many times I long for them to come through the doorway and tell me about their day or have the opportunity to get ready to watch a ballgame with them. What great memories we share!

During their growing years, things seemed so hectic and at times never-ending. But I have learned how quickly time flies. There was a song in the 70s that spoke of the passing of time, and at each passing, the lyrics said, "And I turned around, and they were gone." As long as we live and breathe, that statement will be true. We will turn around, and they will be gone.

The Bible says, "...What is the nature of your life? You are [really] but a wisp of vapor (a puff of smoke, a mist) that is visible for a little while and then disappears [into thin air]" (James 4:14 AMP). Friend, take each day with your children and cherish it. Relish the time you have. Make as many memories as you possibly can. They are quickly growing up before your very eyes. And there is no rewind button to get the time back.

ALAN AND THE FENCE
Understanding Your Ultimate Goal As a Parent

Benjamin Franklin once stated: "Few things help a man more than to give him responsibility and let him know you trust him." This definitely rang true in the life of our son, Alan.

When he was a young boy, Alan often "helped" his dad put up fences around our newly created pastures. I use the word "help" loosely as my husband's idea of him "helping" was Alan handing him the tools. This was really "cool" when Alan was young. But as he got older, we noticed he began to avoid "helping" dad more and more. Once he became a teen, he was anxious to be treated as a man, not a child. Interestingly, an opportunity eventually presented itself in which he got that chance.

One day we received a phone call from a friend. He sadly informed us that his neighbor was dying of cancer, and one of his neighbor's requests was that he take care of his horse. Our friend gladly accepted, but he soon discovered that he needed to fence off about fifteen acres of pasture in order to do it. That prompted him to call us for help.

As in times past, my husband asked Alan to come "help" him with the fence. In light of the situation, he willingly accepted. When they arrived at the job site, they were greeted by the owner and several willing volunteers who had no idea how to run poles and string barbed wire to create a horse pasture. It quickly became apparent that Alan would be needed to do more than merely hand his father tools. To expedite the project most efficiently, they divided into two groups. Alan took one group to one end of the property, while Don took the other to the opposite end.

With complete confidence and know-how, Alan began showing the men how to build the fence. It was a tedious ordeal as they used a tractor and a pole digger to place the poles in the ground in a straight line. With two teams working diligently, they were able to string a lot of fencing that day, but they were not able to finish. The next weekend, they were to meet again to complete the project and hang the gates.

Unfortunately, the weather turned cold and snowy. As I prepared breakfast the morning the work was to resume, I expressed my disappointment to Alan over the weather. "It sure is a shame that the weather is going to prohibit your work on the fence," I said as he was in the next room. To my surprise he came in the kitchen dressed warmly to finish the job.

"Oh no, mom," he said with determination. "We've got to get that fence up. It's not an option. They need to get that horse moved right away."

Due to unforeseen circumstances, Don was not able to help finish the job. That meant the men were counting on Alan to lead them in finishing the fence. And finish the fence they did! When Alan returned home that day, he came back as a man. He had been given a man's responsibility, and he earned the respect of a man for completing a man's job. No one there regarded Alan as a teenager. He was regarded as a man who knew what he was doing.

Friend, your teens have to be given the tools and the opportunities to show what they know. The fact is if you have been training them up in the way they should go, they are very knowledgeable and capable of greater responsibility. They deserve your trust. I encourage you to carefully and prayerfully look for opportunities to extend your trust and allow them to be responsible. God only knows what they can achieve if you will give them a chance and believe!

Endnotes

[1]John C. Maxwell, *Breakthrough Parenting* (Colorado Springs, CO: Focus on the Family Publishing, 1996) p. 194.

Reflection and Application

1. Have you ever confessed and sincerely apologized to your children for something you did (or didn't do) that was not in their best interest? If so, what was their response? How did humbling yourself before them influence their behavior and change your relationship?

    _____

    _____

    _____

    Did you know that saying "I'm sorry" and confessing your faults is something God wants you to do? According to James 5:16, what can you expect to happen in your relationship when you humble yourself and apologize to your kids?

2. The third step toward developing a new game plan for your parenting is to welcome the Lord into your parent-child relationship. If you have done this before, how did it affect your relationship and the atmosphere of your home? If you have never done this, there is no time like the present to begin! Make it a part of your daily prayer.

    _____

    _____

    _____

    God longs to be welcomed in your life. If you draw near to Him, He will draw near to you. You have His Word on it! See Revelation 3:20; James 4:8; Psalm 145:18-19.

3. Believing in your child is very important. It helps prepare and lead them to the next stage of their life. Stop and think. *In what ways do I show my child that I believe in them? What kind of things do I say and do to encourage their God-given gifts and talents to flourish?* Write what comes to mind. Is there any room for improvement?

    _____

    _____

    _____

    Take time to pray and listen to what God speaks to your heart. Write down what He reveals. His words are priceless!

About the Author

PEGGY HUGHES is an author, speaker, and Licensed Professional Counselor (LPC). She is the co-founder of Genesis Christian Counseling in St. Louis, Missouri and holds a Masters of Education in Counseling from the University of Missouri-St. Louis (UMSL). She has also completed two undergraduate degrees from William Jewell College in Psychology and Business Administration and serves as a certified Christian conciliator.

Since 2002, Peggy has been counseling, specializing in marriage and family therapy, including parenting issues. She also specializes in adult survivors of child abuse. Along with the one-hour counseling approach, she does a lot of work with highly conflicted relationships through an intensive counseling and conciliation format. Peggy and her daughter, Stephanie, use horses in Equine Assisted Counseling to help people deal with personal struggles in their lives.

Peggy has served as President for the Missouri Mental Health Counselor's Association (MMHCA). She currently serves on the Advisory Board for Gateway Christian Broadcasting Company (99.1 JOYFM radio), St. Louis, Mo.

In addition to being a stay-at-home mom during her children's developing years, Peggy also served five years in law enforcement. She and her husband, Don, have been married over thirty-five years, are the parents of two grown children, and have two grandchildren. They reside in Hillsboro, Missouri.

Contact Peggy at…

Genesis Christian Counseling, LLC
2190 S. Mason Rd., Suite 306
St. Louis, Mo. 63131

phughes.genesis@gmail.com
www.genesischristiancounseling.org